9780998861685
T0819552

BARAGOUIN

This artist's book, BARAGOUIN, is a companion piece to a video installation of the same name.

The video work BARAGOUIN, filmed in a now-closed commercial showroom in Los Angeles, presents copies of sculptures that maintain vague resemblances to their originals and influences, ranging in style from Buddhist to Rococo to Neoclassical to Modernist. These sculptures appear to speak in voices that bear the traces of each figure's imagined provenance.

BARAGOUIN, the book, catalogs these sculptures and their imagined art-historical provenance based on morphological resemblances, and documents the cacophony of their constructed voices—a pastiche of verbal nonsense, inscribed through the place-holder language of 'Greek text' and phonetically imitated sounds of languages from around the world.

BARAGOUIN

A NONSENSE OPERA

baragouin
noun
ba·ra·gouin | \ ¦barə¦gwa^{n} \
outlandish unintelligible speech : jargon

KIM SCHOEN

PROVENANCE
EDWARD STERRETT

SOUND DESIGN
MANUELA SCHININÁ

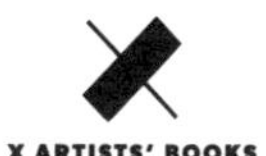

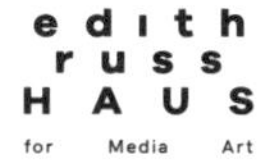

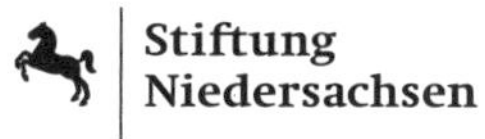

“Alles Verborgene sieht das Geschäft.” (Everything hidden sees the business.)

—DIE SCHAMHAFTIGKEIT (PUDEUR)
ID #38

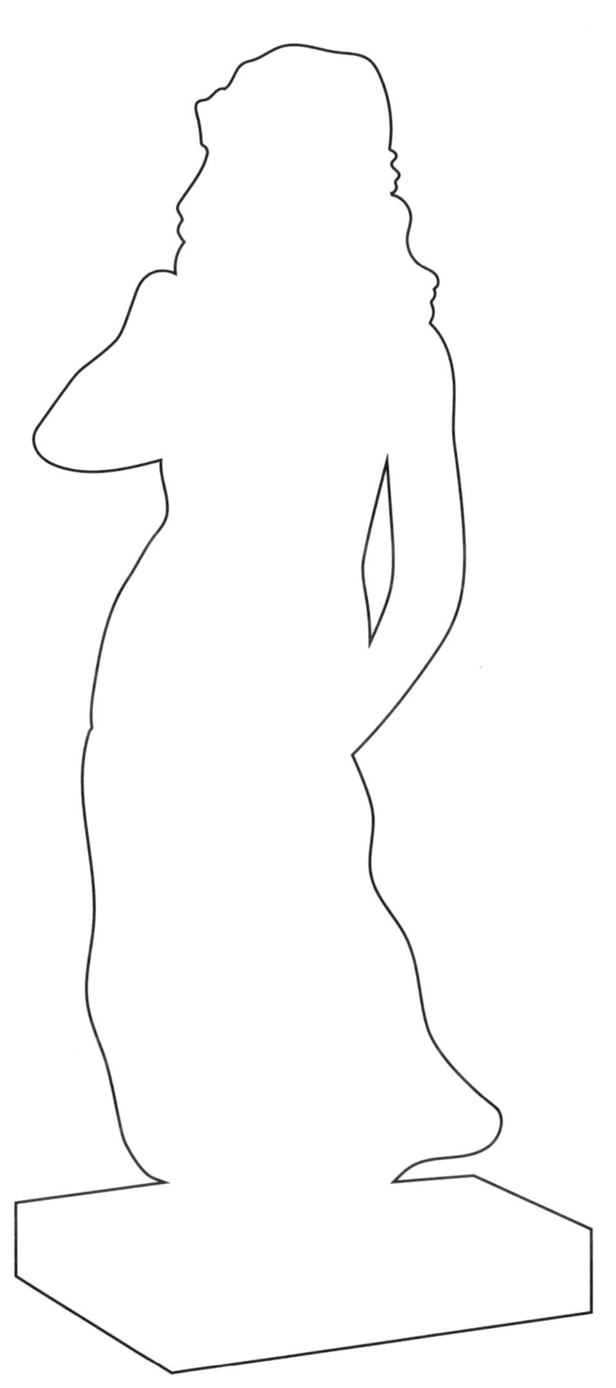

CONTENTS

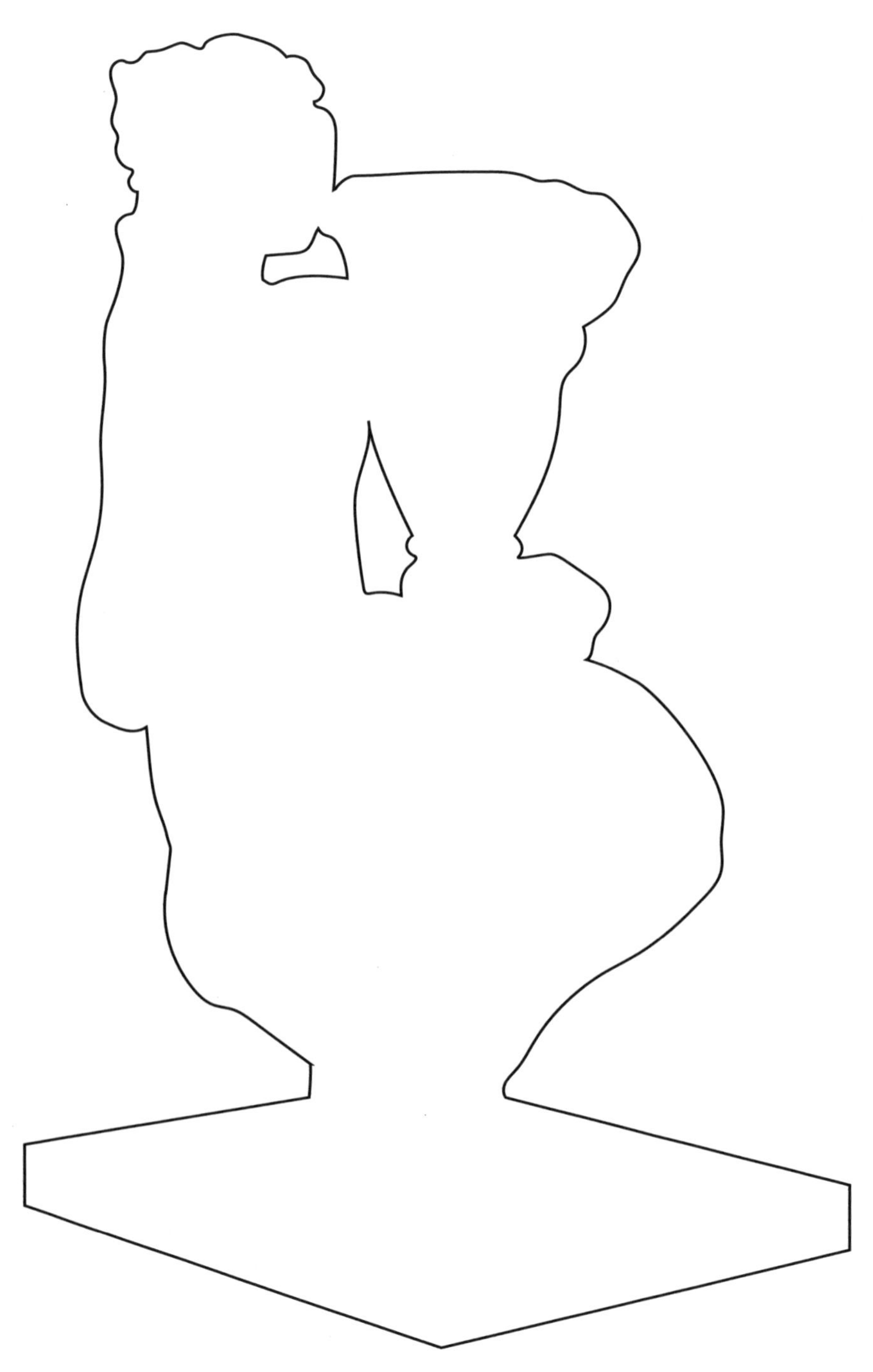

“Η αντιστροφή
αφήνει το
υποτιθέμενο
παπούτσι σε
αντάλλαγμα
για όχι
καινούριο.”

(The
reversal
leaves the
supposed shoe
in exchange
for not new.)

—NAIAD
ID #8

IDENTIFICATION KEY

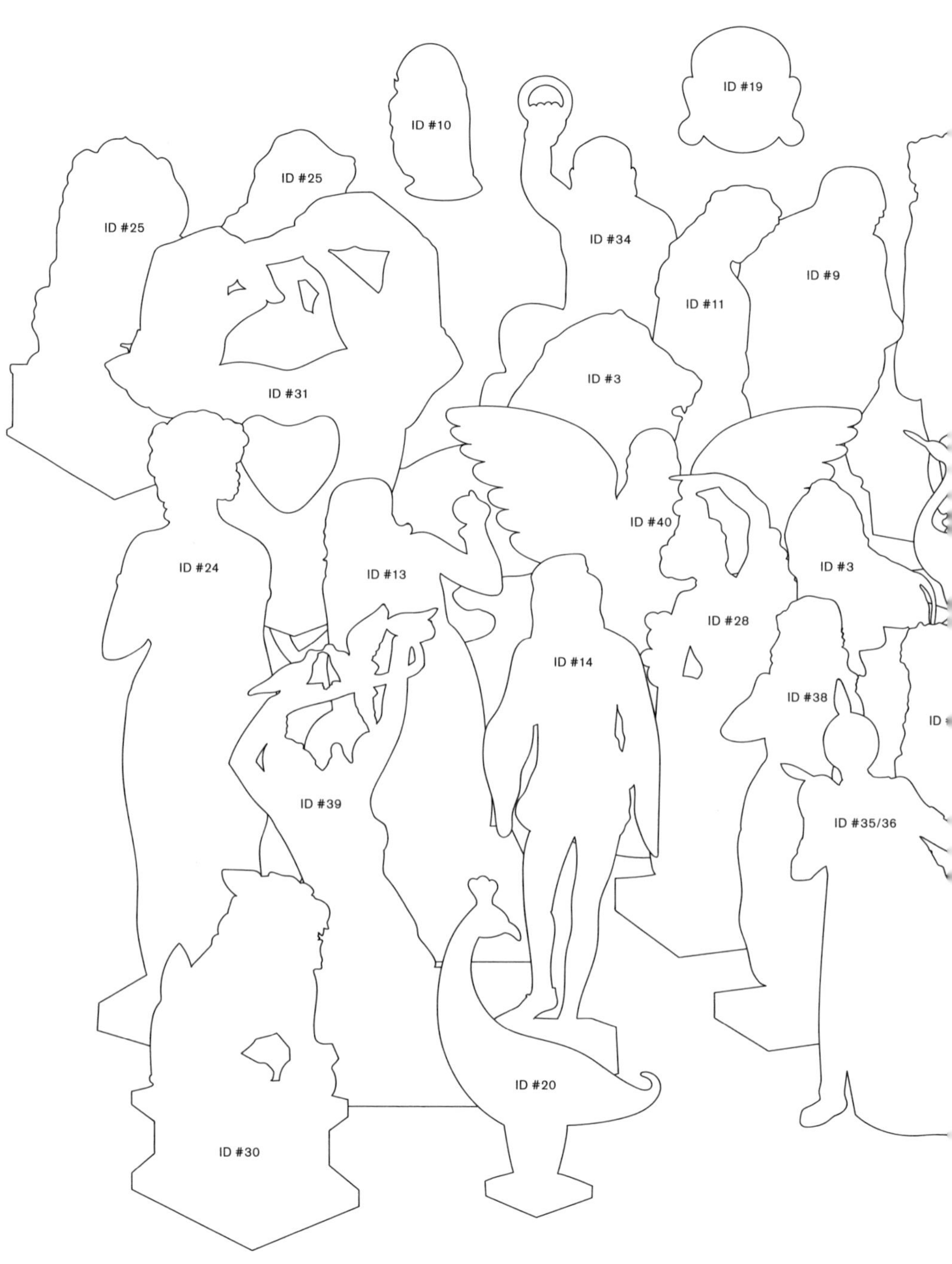
ID #19
ID #10
ID #25
ID #25
ID #34
ID #9
ID #11
ID #3
ID #31
ID #40
ID #3
ID #24
ID #13
ID #28
ID #14
ID #38
ID #35/36
ID #39
ID #20
ID #30

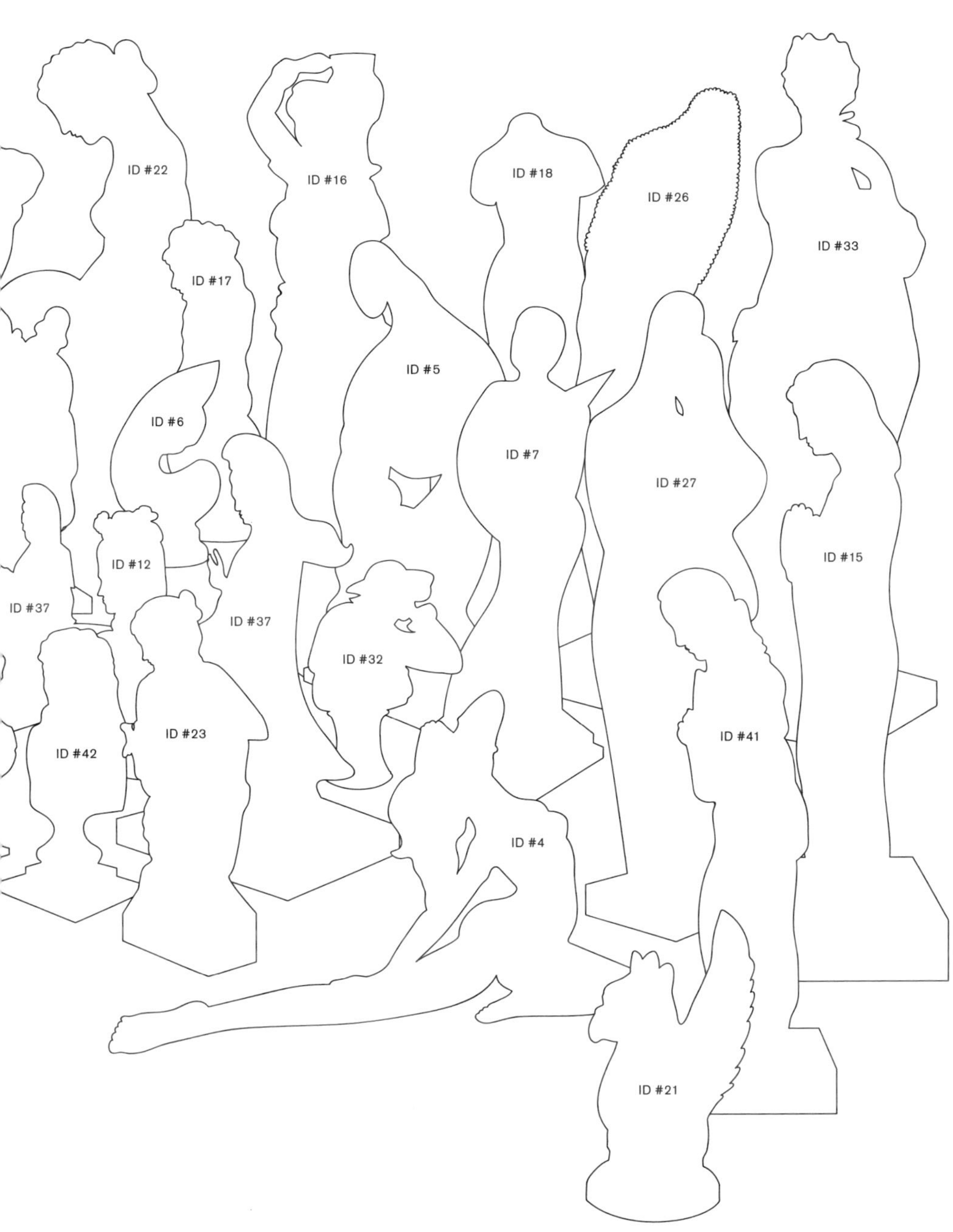
ID #22
ID #16
ID #18
ID #26
ID #33
ID #17
ID #5
ID #6
ID #7
ID #27
ID #15
ID #12
ID #37
ID #37
ID #32
ID #23
ID #42
ID #41
ID #4
ID #21

ID #1
Possibly Marie Antoinette

ID #2
Bust Man, River God

ID #3
Lions (Indoor)

ID #4
Nymph

ID #5
Mother with Child

ID #6
Female Ornament

ID #7
Modern-esque

ID #8
Neo-Classical Nymph,
Naiad, or Danaid

ID #9
The Thinker

ID #10
Guan Yin (Bodhisattva)

ID #11
Woman with Drape

ID #12
Portrait Bust of
Aristocratic Woman

ID #13
Temptation of Eve

ID #14
Renaissance Page
Boy Bringing a
Cardinal a Letter

ID #15
Praying Woman

ID #16
Woman with Vase

ID #17
Putto, Cherub

ID #18
Aphrodite of Knidos

ID #19
Laughing Buddha,
Budai, or Hotei in Japan

ID #20
Peacock

ID #21
Griffin

ID #22
Seated Danaid

ID #23
Woman with Birds

ID #24
Woman with Flowers

ID #25
Lions (Outdoor)

ID #26
Abstract Undress

ID #27
The Embrace

ID #28
Aphrodite Anadyomene

ID #29
Crane

ID #30
Fu Dogs

ID #31
The Ring

ID #32
Dutch Boy

ID #33
Allegorical Figure

ID #34
Fuhu Luohan

ID #35/36
Wagnerians

ID #37
Guan Yin
(Compassionate Mother)

ID #38
die Schamhaftigkeit
(Pudeur)

ID #39
Nude Fielding
Birds

ID #40
Angel

ID #41
Woman with
Wheat

ID #42
Bust After Bach

ID #43
Laughing Buddhas
(Seated)

PROVENANCE

EDWARD STERRETT

ID #1 POSSIBLY MARIE ANTOINETTE

Busts of Marie Antoinette (1755–1793),[1,2] Madame du Barry (1743–1793), and other esteemed (or infamous) ladies of the courts of Louis XV and Louis XVI adorn the Petit Trianon at the Palace of Versailles. As mistresses to kings, most of them were sent to the guillotine during the French Revolution. More of these busts appeared in a restoration of the Queen's Grove in the gardens at Versailles in the late 19th century,[3] when revivals of Louis XV and Louis XVI styles in the decorative arts were mobilized in the service of nationalist and imperialist ambitions. During this time there was also a massive resurgence in the production of Sèvres porcelain copies of these busts.

ID #1 1 2 3

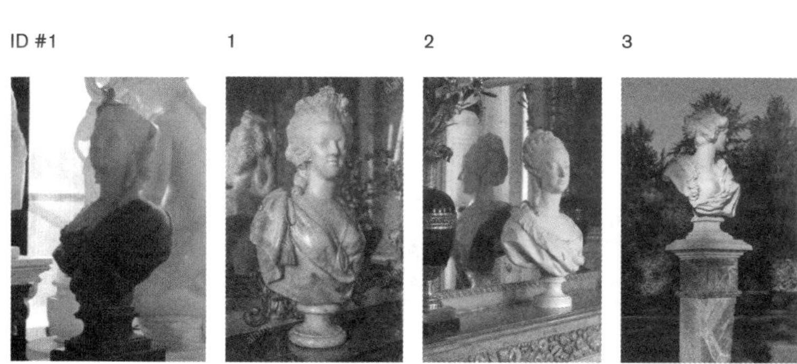

ID #2

BUST MAN, RIVER GOD

The attributes of this figure—laurel crown, flowing beard, furrowed brow, face turned down to one side—combined with its presentation on a small turned pedestal, suggest a prototype in the Italian Baroque reinterpretations of the Greco-Roman classical tradition. It is likely modeled on a river god, one of the lower level gods of the Greek mythological tradition, typically named after the natural features that they protect. Major Italian prototypes include the River Ganges depicted in Bernini's (1598–1680) *Fontana dei Quattro Fiumi* (1651),[1] in Rome, or more distantly his *Neptune and Triton* (1622–3), now at the Victoria and Albert Museum in London; Giambologna (1529–1608) also depicted the River Ganges in a sculpture for the Oceanus fountain on the Isolotto in the Boboli Gardens. Giambologna's sculpture served as a reference for an even more closely related sculpture, Jean-Jacques Caffieri's (1725–1792) *A River God* (1759),[2] which was his reception piece at the Royal French Academy; it is now in the collection of the Louvre. One rarely sees river gods depicted in a bust format, though one attributed to Caffieri and based on a different sculpture was sold out of the Gustav Rau collection at a Sotheby's auction in 2013. Another *Bust of a River God* (1798),[3] attributed to Louis-Simon Boizot (1743–1809), and clearly influenced by Caffieri's, is now in the collection at LACMA.

ID #2 1 2 3

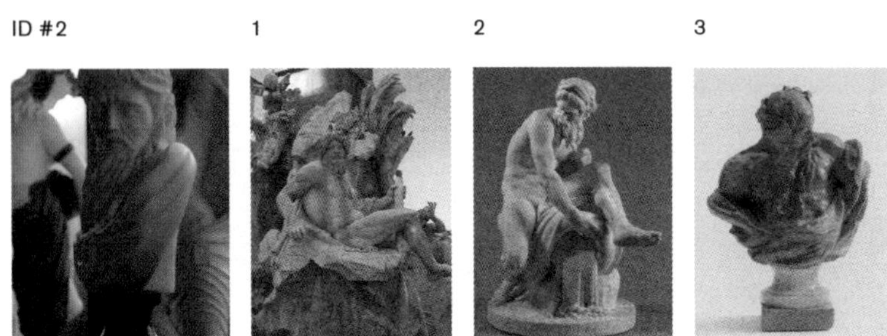

ID #3

LIONS (INDOOR)

The Medici lions, originally displayed at the Villa Medici in Rome and now at the Loggia dei Lanzi in Florence, are probably the most iconic twin lion statues in the Western tradition. One is an ancient Roman sculpture dating to the 2nd century CE. The other is a 16th century copy by Flaminio Vacca.[1] Each famously places their outer front paw on a globe, an ancient symbol signifying worldly domination, and their heads are turned slightly downward toward them in acknowledgment. The globes do not feature in this first pair of *Baragouin Lions,* but can be seen in a different pair visible in an exterior shot (ID #25). Although the Medici lions' mouths are open, they are more expressive of stately composure than ferocity as is the case in the *Baragouin Lions.*

The roaring lion doesn't seem to emerge widely in statuary in the European tradition until the late until the late 19th and early 20th centuries, typically in statues related to monuments of war, and rarely if ever in pairs. Although in the Chinese tradition, pairs of guardian lions (also called fu dogs or fu lions in English) are often depicted with their mouths open, they tend to be seated and much more stylized in their formal characteristics, as can be seen in another later exterior shot in *Baragouin* (ID #30).

The Paseo del Prado lions,[2] made in the 1920s in Cuba, match the stance and open mouth of this set of *Baragouin Lions* most precisely, although the mane is of a significantly different texture. The Prado lions are made of bronze, which was melted down from the cannons that protected the city in the 16th and 17th centuries.

ID #3 | 1 | 2

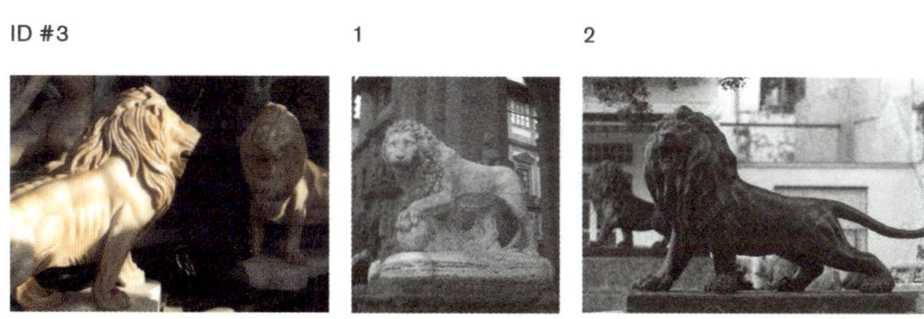

ID #4

NYMPH

There is no specific prototype for this sculpture in the art historical canon, but the eroticized arabesque posture, accentuated by elongated limbs and high perky bust, recalls the many depictions of Nereids and orientalized erotic dancers by 19th-century French symbolist painter Gaston Bussiere. One might also think of the work of William-Adolphe Bouguereau, who frequently took up similar subject matter; although, his female nudes tend to have a more softened, less dynamic musculature. It would not be surprising to find this posture modeled somewhere in the cyclone of nudes depicted in his *Les Oreades* (1902).[1] For a strange counterpoint, consider Bouguereau's *Dante and Virgil* (1850),[2] which features a stormy homoerotic battle scene in the eighth circle of hell. The arched back, raised chest, flung back head and arms, and bent under front knee of the man on the bottom, are weirdly reminiscent of the back-bending *Baragouin Nymph*, though with an almost completely inverted thematic valence.

In the 21st century, such poses invariably call up visions of erotic dance, particularly pole dancing, which has enjoyed a resurgence as a popular exercise and competitive acrobatic dance form in the last decade.

ID #4 1 2

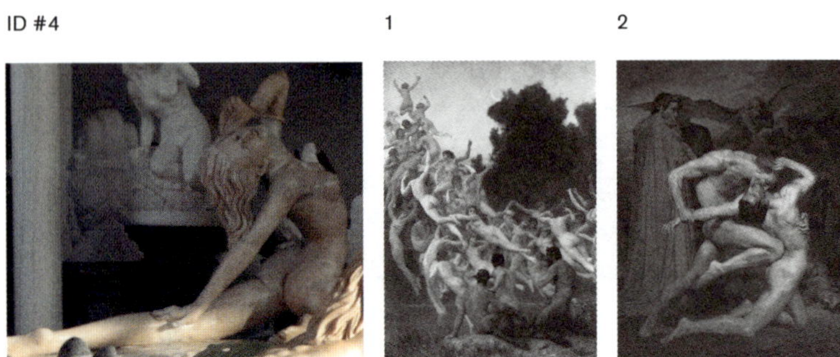

ID #5 MOTHER WITH CHILD

This figure is a typical example of a late 20th-century popular style that might best be described as *modern-esque*: a universalizing, softened figuration which borrows from the biomorphic primitivism of sculptors such as Jean (Hans) Arp (1886–1966),[1] Barbara Hepworth (1903–1975),[2] and Henry Moore (1898–1986), transposing these into a slightly blunted sentimental key. The strong emphasis of the bust in the *Baragouin* figure offers a novel interpretation of the underlying symbology of the fertility goddess, which can be traced back to the Cycladic tradition, c. 4000–4500 BCE, from which much of this strain of modernist primitivism draws. A much more ancient example can be found in the famous Venus of Willendorf,[3] made between 22,000 and 24,000 BCE.

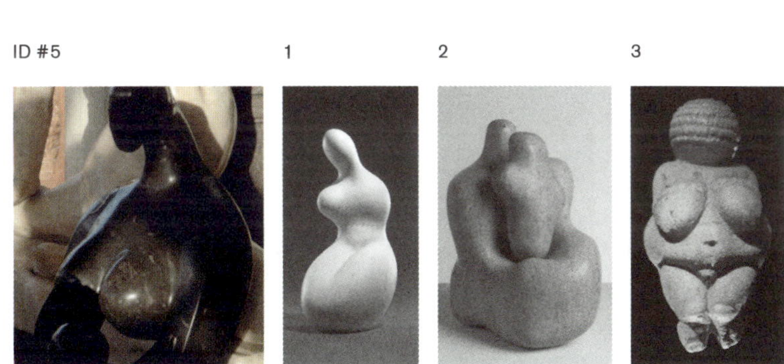

ID #5 1 2 3

ID #6

FEMALE ORNAMENT

This ornamental fragment lacks any specific prototype, but it is strongly influenced by the Euro-American Art Nouveau style, which emerged in the decades of 1890–1910. The inclusion of a distorted scroll or volute which serves as the base of a petal-like form encasing the head emphasizes the vegetalization of classical forms characteristic of a certain strain of the Art Nouveau impulse. One would typically find this kind of sculpture as an architectural ornament attached directly to a cornice at the corner of a building,[1] or in an overdoor.[2] The use of female figures in architectural ornament dates back to archaic Greece and Phoenicia. First described as Caryatides by Vitruvius in *De Architectura*, 1st century BCE, the most famous early examples form the columns of the Erechtheion on the Acropolis in Athens, Greece. Caryatids are named after the ancient Peloponnesian town Karyai, which was famous in the ancient world for its temple dedicated to the Goddess Artemis, who was worshipped by the town's women in a form of ritual ecstatic dance. According to Vitruvius, the women were subjected to slavery by the Athenians after siding with the Persians in the Greco-Persian wars, and their use as architectural ornament is a sign of their bondage. The *Baragouin* ornament is free standing and mounted on a pedestal, which lends it a degree of autonomy suggestive of modernist sculpture, such as the work of Czech artist Joseph Martinek.[3]

ID #6 1 2 3

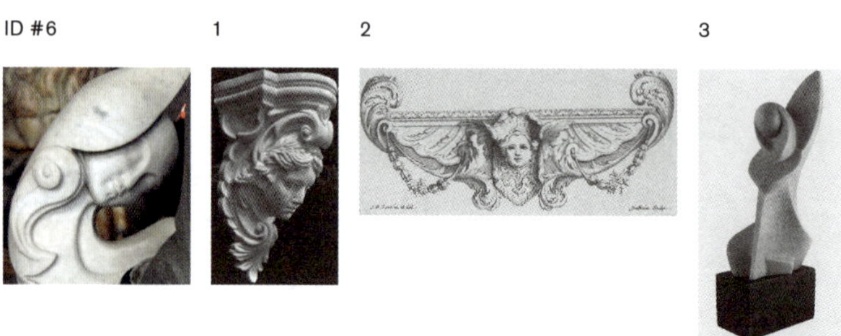

ID #7

MODERN-ESQUE

This is another strong example of what I have previously termed *modern-esque* (see ID #5). In this case, the edition of a starkly geometric triangular mass tucked under one arm and across the torso of the figure suggests some kind of stringed instrument—a guitar, or a lute, perhaps? It also recalls a form of neo-Art Deco postmodern pastiche that emerged in the early 1980s which conflated the soft holistic forms of the modern-esque, the markedly angular geometries of the conventional Art-Deco style, and the graphic effects of alternating bold monotones with dappled and speckled surfaces. One might think of the Patrick Nagel's *Commemorative #1* (1984),[1] or Peter Shire's *Brazil Side Table* from the *Memphis* series.[2]

ID #7

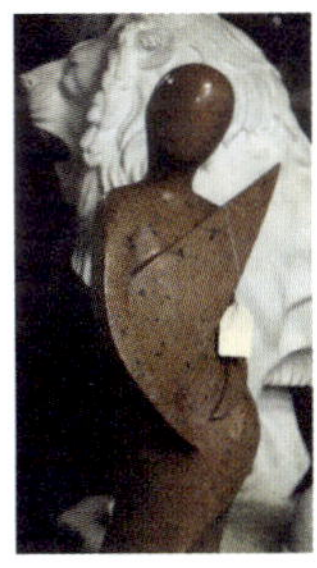

1

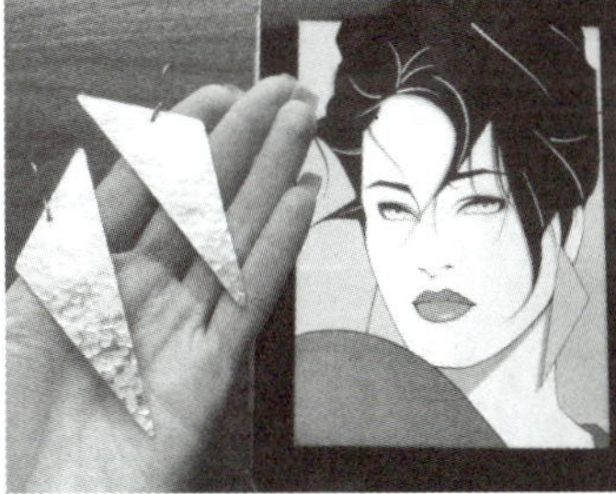

2

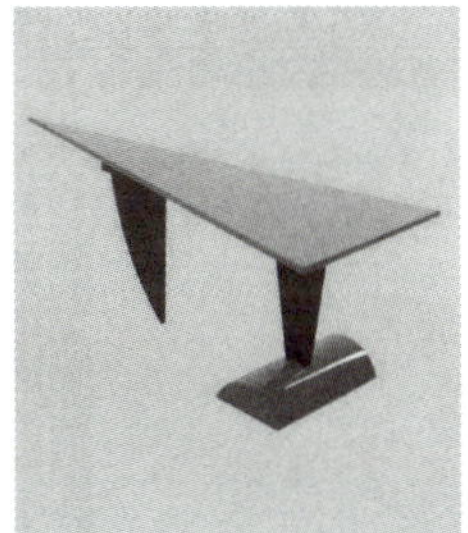

ID #8

NEO-CLASSICAL NYMPH, NAIAD, OR DANAID

The half draped himation (a particular cut and fold of toga) exposing this figure's bare shoulder,[1] combined with the oversized acanthus ornamentation on the vase which she holds, lend a distinctly classicizing character typical of 19th-century Euro-American Neoclassicism, while the delicately defined musculature of the exposed shoulder and back are peculiarly modern. Renaissance and Neoclassical statues of figures holding urns or vases are typically allegorical representations of springs, streams, and rivers.[2] One of the early interpretations of the Venus de Milo suggested that she may be holding a large vase in a similar manner, which would have identified the sculpture as a Danaid—one of the fifty daughters of Danaos, all but one of who killed their husbands on their wedding night, and were thus condemned to carry water in leaky vessels for eternity.

ID #8 | 1 | 2

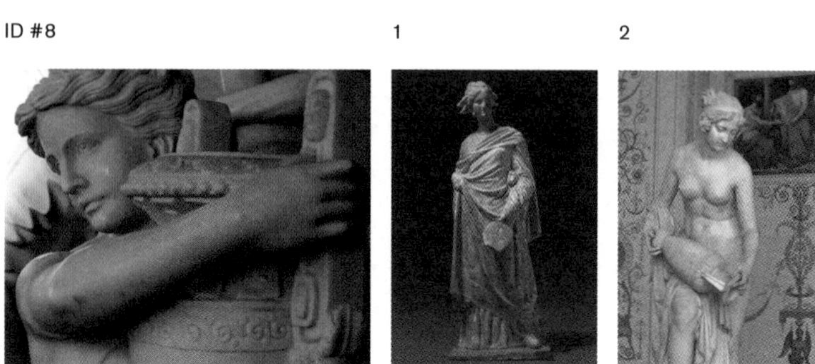

ID #9

THE THINKER

Although art historians recognize 28 copies of Rodin's *The Thinker* cast in bronze directly under the artist's supervision, and though they are cast in different sizes and from different molds, it is generally agreed that the only prototype is in the artist's mind. Originally designed to represent Dante contemplating the fate of the damned in a larger sculptural work representing the *Gates of Hell* (which remained unfinished in Rodin's lifetime),[1] *The Thinker* was exhibited separately beginning in 1904 in Paris and at the St. Louis World's Fair, where it shed its direct allegorical association with Dante and became an icon of modern sculpture.[2] It subsequently became popular, particularly with American collectors, and was recast on a commission basis throughout Rodin's life. It was almost immediately taken up in the popular media for caricature, where its status as a great work of art was reinforced precisely because it was so worthy of satirical appropriation. It has withstood repeated re-appropriations ever since.[3]

ID #9 | 1 | 2 | 3

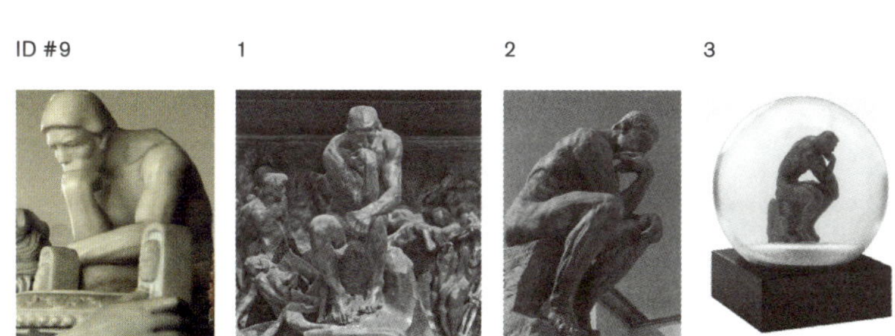

ID #10 GUAN YIN (BODHISSATVA)

The prototype for this figure is Guan Yin Bodhisattva, a female bodhisattva who is the personification of universal compassion in Chinese Buddhism, also called Avalokiteśvara in Sanskrit. The softened facial features, vertical disposition, and draped crown with an inset figure in lotus posture are characteristic of Ming dynasty statuary representing Guan Yin, particularly the white porcelain statuary of He Chaozong manufactured at the Dehua kilns in Fujian province in the 17th century.[1] A similar style emerged in Japanese interpretations of Guan Yin known as Kwannon or Kannon, most notably a version known as Jibo Kannon, compassionate mother Kannon, which represents Kannon as a mother holding a child,[2] and was also widely used for Christian worship when overt Christian iconography was officially suppressed during the Tokugawa shogunate. Deep prototypes include a 3rd-century Gandaharan statue of Avalokiteśvara (now at the Musée Guimet in Paris),[3] which may be the earliest surviving example to include the crown with inset figure in lotus posture.

ID #10 1 2 3

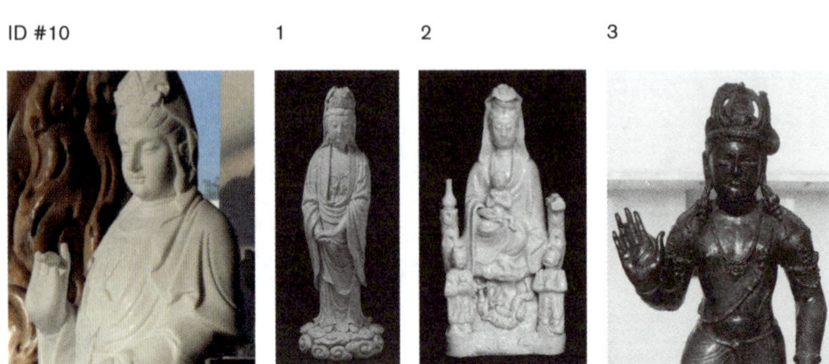

ID #11

WOMAN WITH DRAPE

The posture of this figure can be identified as the posture of modesty in the classical tradition: one hand reaching to cover the bosom and the other to cover the genitals. This immediately suggests the ancient prototype of Praxiteles' *Aphrodite of Knidos*. The hair pulled back from the temples is typical of many copies after Praxiteles, but in this case the profusion of locks extending down the back and shoulder recall the Capitoline Venus in particular,[1] although the *Baragouin* figure's posture is reversed in comparison; she looks to the right and raises her left hand to her bosom. The presence of the drape entwined around her arm draws on a famous copy by Canova now in the Palazzo Piti,[2] but the coloring is a purely modern interpretation.

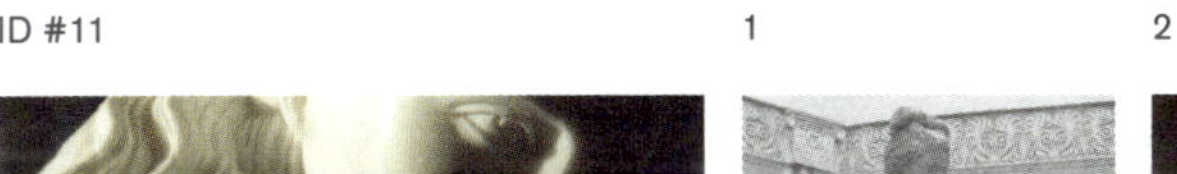

ID #11

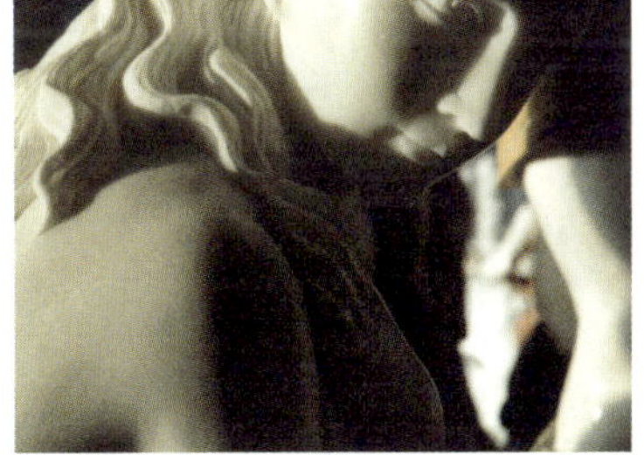

1

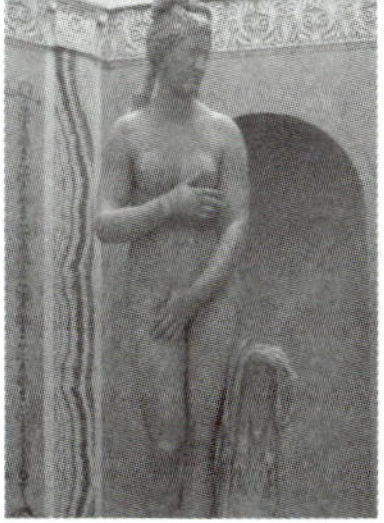

2

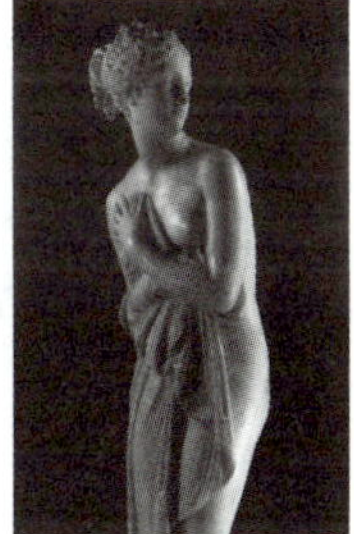

ID #12

PORTRAIT BUST OF ARISTOCRATIC WOMAN

This is another French aristocratic bust, quite similar to ID #1 *Possibly Marie Antoinette,* although viewed in profile one notices the rather strange treatment of the hair, which suggests that it is a rough attempt to copy a Sèvres manufactured bust of Madame du Barry (1743–1793),[1] a copy of which is now in the collection of the Metropolitan Museum in New York. One might also look to the bust of Marie Antoinette in the dining room of the Petit Trianon,[2] although the curls are less severe in this example. The choice of clothing in the *Baragouin* bust is closer to later busts of Marie Antoinette, which tend to have significantly more fabric above the shoulder. The facial features are not easy to judge, but they are more in keeping with the marble bust of Madame du Barry by Augustin Pajou (1730–1809),[3] now at the Louvre Museum in Paris. Pajou also executed the mold for the Sevres bust. The slight downturn of the face in the *Baragouin* copy would be completely out of place in 18th-century portrait busts of the aristocracy, where you typically find an elegantly lifted chin.

ID #12 | 1 | 2 | 3

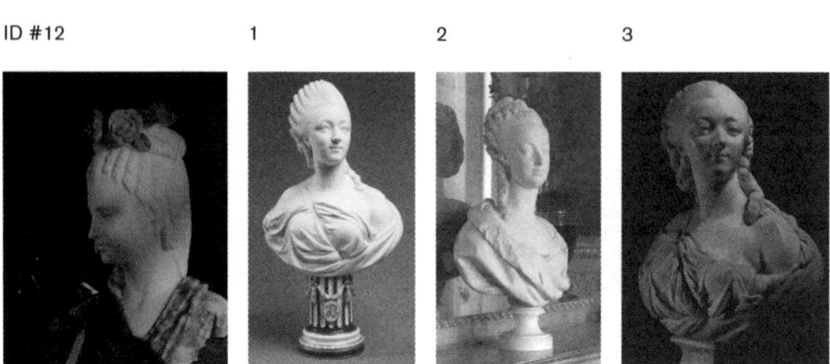

ID #13

TEMPTATION OF EVE

Although it is not unusual to figure Eve clutching an apple in one hand while she braces herself with the other, in these cases she is typically depicted in a classical contra-posto. In statuary, she is never depicted in the kind of hunched and unbalanced posture that she assumes in the *Baragouin Eve*. One would have to look to the history of painting to find a feasible prototype. And while nothing quite compares to the awkwardness of the *Baragouin Eve*, the most likely prototypes are Peter Paul Rubens' *Adam and Eve* (1628–29),[1] in the Museo del Prado in Madrid, and its predecessor, *The Fall of Man* (1550) by Titian,[2] also in the Prado. Rubens' painting is very nearly a perfect copy in terms of the postures of the figures and the overall composition. Both depict Eve unbalanced by her reach as she braces herself with the other hand on a tree limb. The combination of Adam reaching up from below in alarm, and the slight angle of the primary trunk of the tree, counter-balance Eve's dramatic posture in a way which is impossible in a sculptural representation of Eve alone. The hairstyle is not of the period.[3]

ID #13 | 1 | 2 | 3

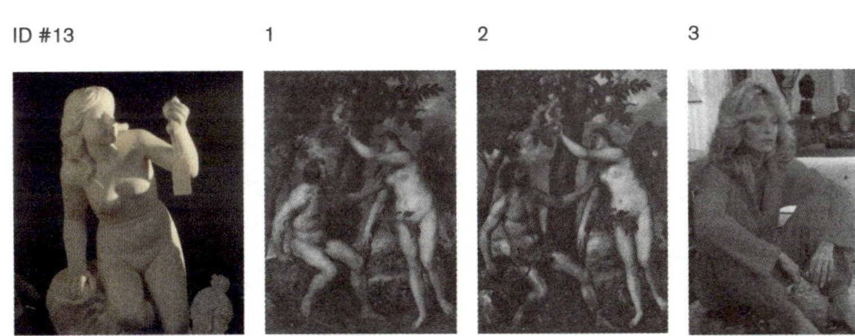

ID #14

RENAISSANCE PAGE BOY BRINGING A CARDINAL A LETTER

There is very little visual evidence to work from in the case of this figure. We have only the flat round hat, a style which is typically found on men in Italian Renaissance paintings. These kinds of hats would have been worn by men in all stations of society, so it is not a particularly strong signal of any specific identity. A great number of Renaissance portraits of young men wearing a similar style of hat (always in red) have been attributed to Sandro Boticelli (1445–1510). Particularly fine examples include *Portrait of a Young Man* (1480–85),[1] now at the National Gallery in London, and *Portrait of a Youth* (1482–5),[2] now at the National Gallery in Washington D.C. The latter picture has become particularly popular as an internet meme in the 21st century because the figure seems to be displaying a hand sign used by gangs to signify identification with the westside of a city. A slightly different version of the cap can be found in Domenico Ghirlandaio's (1448–1494) *Portrait of Francesco Sassetti and His Son Teodoro* (1488), now at the Met in New York.

ID #14 1 2

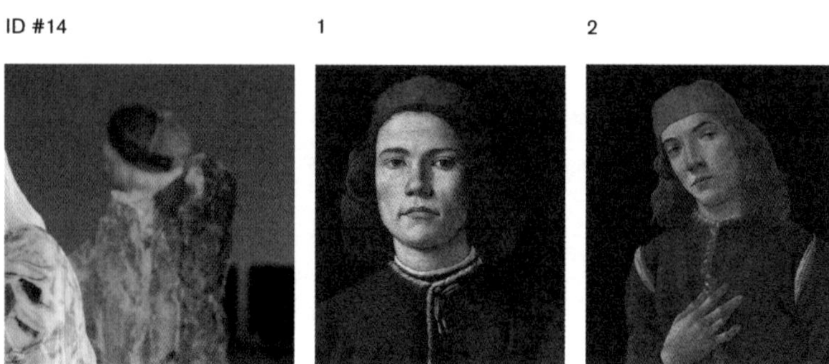

ID #15

PRAYING WOMAN

Although very little of the *Baragouin Praying Woman* is visible, a female figure in loose robes with head slightly bowed and hands in prayer is so ubiquitous in Christian iconography that it is not too speculative to suggest that the deep prototype for this particular figure can be found in the jamb statuary of French Gothic cathedrals,[1] where Christian Iconography first takes the form of statuary in the round (or very nearly in the round). However, a specific jamb figure is difficult to pinpoint, as most of these figures are represented with one arm raised and the other lowered, and they tend to be clutching attributes, such as scepters, books, even the baby Jesus. We are thus drawn to another pole in the constellation of prototypes, which is the Renaissance iconography of the Madonna with head bowed and hands in prayer. Here useful early examples can be found in the low relief sculptures of Donatello (1386–1466), such as *Virgin and Child with Four Cherubs* (1440–1450) in the Staatliche Museum in Berlin,[2] and the *Madonna and Child* (1450) at the Victoria and Albert Museum in London. A notable early example is by Albrecht Dürer (1471–1528). The exposed hair of the *Baragouin Praying Woman* suggests a more modern sensibility, but it is not clear whether this characteristic corresponds to a specific later prototype or is simply an artifact of the *Baragouin* copy.

ID #15

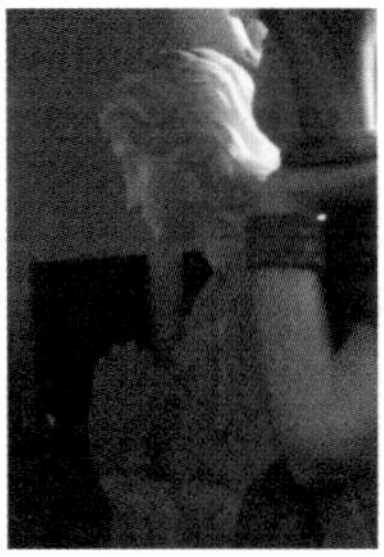

1

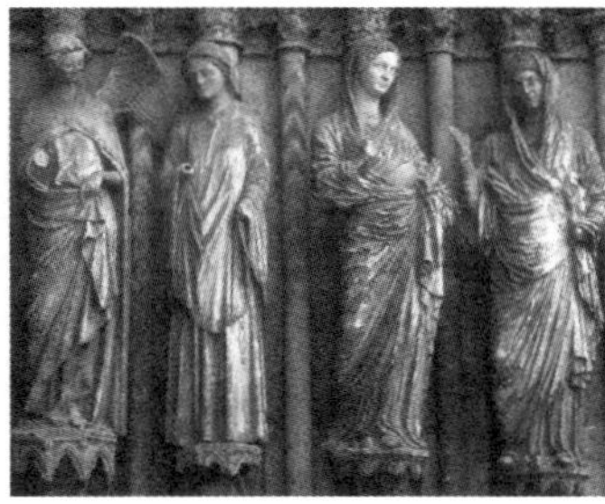

2

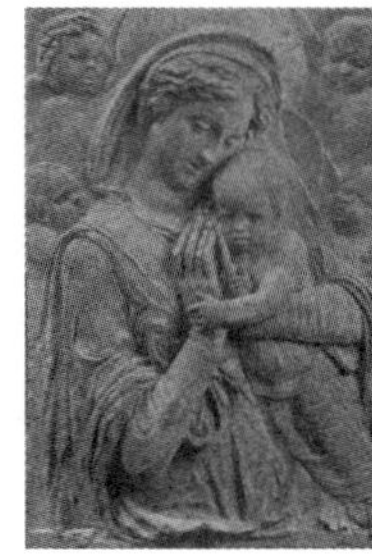

ID #16

WOMAN WITH VASE

This figure is a variation on the theme of the Danaid. Drawn from Greek Mythology, the Danaides were daughters of Danaos, all but one of whom killed their husbands on their wedding night, and were thus condemned to carry water in leaky vessels for eternity. Early representations of Danaides are visible in Attic pottery,[1] but the dominant later iconography typically refers to a widely reproduced image by Pre-Raphaelite John William Waterhouse, *The Danaides* (1903).[2] In this *Baragouin* example, the exposed midriff and prominent arm band lends a 19th-century orientalist cast, which draws on North African and Turkish themes, directing them toward more or less prurient interests, as in the example *Dance of Almeh* (1863) by French painter Jean-Leon Gerome (1824–1904).[3] Indeed, other views of this figure in *Baragouin* show not only an exposed midriff, but the underside of her breasts exposed by the cut of her shirt, a style which was popularized by Christina Aguilera in 2002.

ID #16 1 2 3

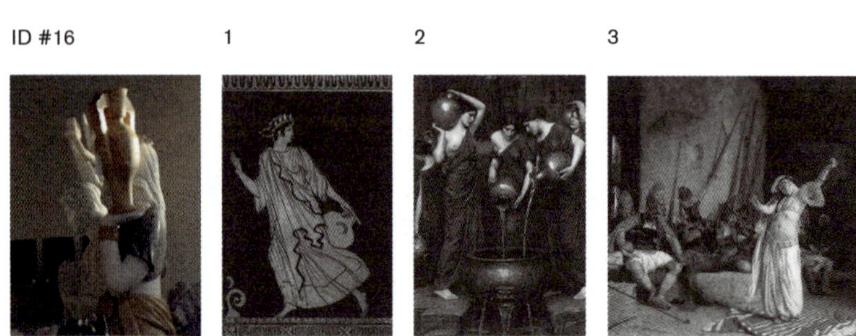

ID #17

PUTTO, CHERUB

Since the 16th century in Europe, Putti have been identified with the Greek god Eros (later Amor in the Roman tradition), the infant god of love. Italian Renaissance artists also assimilated Putti into the Christian tradition where they are associated with the divine Cherub. The origins of this figure are traceable to 2nd-century infant Bacchoi found on Roman sarcophagi.[1] Donatello (1386–1466) is widely credited with the revival of these figures in the European Renaissance, but the Renaissance Putto drew as much from the vernacular figure of the *spiritello* or sprite—a kind of quasi-animist expression of popular spiritualism—as it did from the ancient model of the infant Bacchoi. An example by Donatello that strongly resembles the *Baragouin Putto* in its torqued seated posture is now in the collection of the Musée Jacquemart André in Paris.[2] One remarkable deep prototype is a Hellenistic bronze statue of sleeping Eros, now at the Metropolitan Museum in New York. It represents a theme which was likely copied hundreds of times in the Roman Imperial era, and returned in courtly art of the Renaissance. Putti also became extremely popular in the mid-18th century in France. Étienne-Maurice Falconet (1716–1791) produced a particularly famous example of a freestanding marble statue of seated cupid, titled *Amour Menaçant* (1757),[3] which exists in two copies, one at the Louvre in Paris and the other at the Rijksmuseum in Amsterdam. Ten years after Falconet's sculpture, one of the most scathing and witty remarks ever penned about the proliferation of Putti in European art appears in Denis Diderot's (1713–1784) salon review of Jean Honoré Fragonard's painting *Essaim d'Amours* (1767) in which he describes the painting as "a nice big omelette of children in the sky."[4]

ID #17 1 2

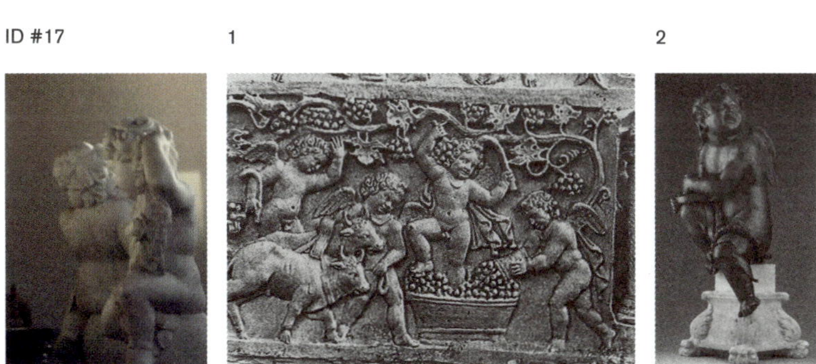

The popular sentimentalization of Putti has continued in the spirit of the French 18th century well into the contemporary period, but by far the most appropriated Putti in the late 20th- and early 21st-century kitsch economy are the cherubs at the bottom of Raphael's *Sistine Madonna* (1512).[5]

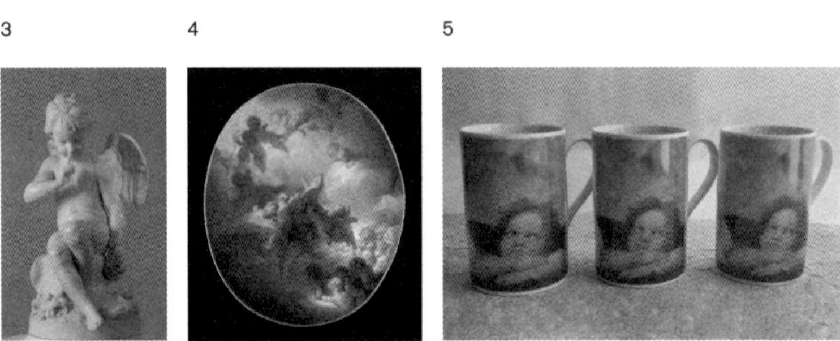

ID #18

APHRODITE OF KNIDOS

The downturned arms and slightly forward tilt of the torso of this figure are characteristic of the Aphrodite of Knidos, who, when she still has her arms, is typically using them to cover herself. A headless, armless version of this statue (also missing her legs from the knee down) is preserved in the Louvre.[1] See ID #11 for more on *Aphrodite of Knidos*.

ID #18

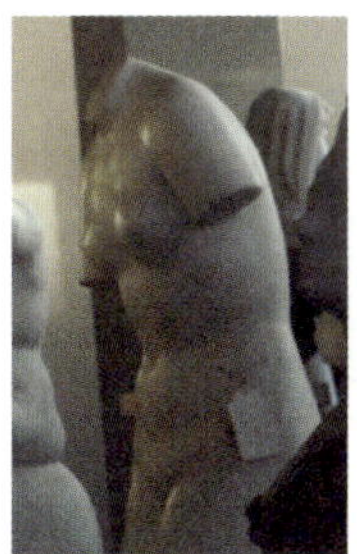

1

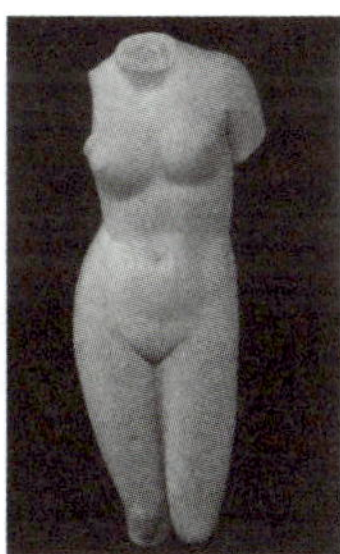

ID #19

LAUGHING BUDDHA, BUDAI, OR HOTEI IN JAPAN

Known as *Laughing Buddha* or *Fat Buddha* because he is typically depicted smiling and with a big belly, Budai was adopted into the Chinese Chan Buddhist tradition in the mid-12th century as a symbol of abundance, and happiness. In the 13th century he became popular in Japan, where he is known as Hotei. He is often mistakenly recognized as the Buddha in the West, but the figure is based on a legendary 10th-century Chinese Buddhist monk.

Depictions of Hotei in mask form come from the Noh tradition of Japanese theater, a form of narrative dance that has been performed since the 14th century. Along with their use in theater productions where they identify specific characters, they are often hung decoratively.[1]

ID #19

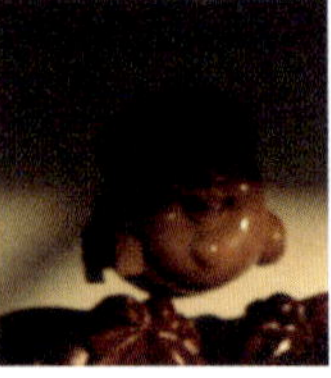

1

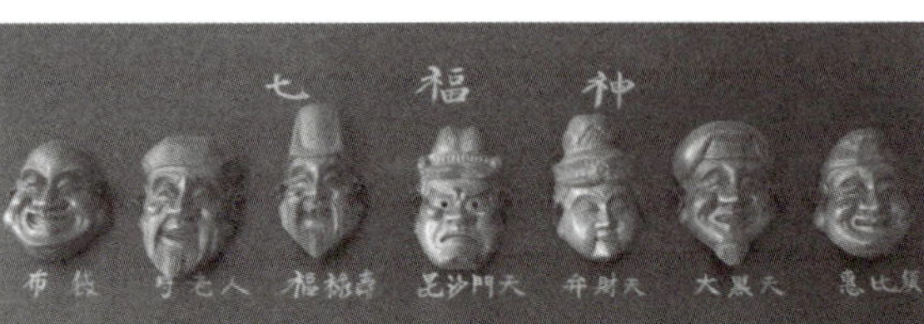

ID #20

PEACOCK

The peacock is an ancient symbol and deployed across many of the world's cultures. In the Hindu tradition, the peacock is the vehicle of Kartikeya, son of Shiva, also known as Skanda and Murugan, or the Peacock Angel, Ta'us Malik in the ancient Yazidi faith, al-Khidr in Islamic and pre-Islamic lore, mentor of Moses in the Quran. The ancient Greeks associated the peacock with eternal life, and the Christian tradition adopted this valence. The ability of the peacock to consume poisonous plants without adverse effects has been credited with this aspect of peacock symbolism, as well as with meanings more aligned with Hindu and Buddhist traditions related to conquering worldly flaws such as greed and desire. In Chinese Buddhism, the peacock became a symbol of the omniscience of the bodhisattva Guan Yin. In this case, the ocular pattern on the peacock's feathers are the primary locus of symbolic meaning. In the Renaissance alchemical tradition, the oily rainbow sheen of the feathers represent the iridescent phase of the transformation of base matter into gold. The iconographic history of the peacock is as rich and varied as its many symbolic meanings, including notable examples of its use in ancient Hindu temple statuary,[1] ancient Roman freestanding bronze sculptures,[2] Byzantine mosaics,[3] Chinese porcelain motifs as well as freestanding bronze statuary,[4] 17th-century Netherlandish painting,[5] not to mention manuscript illumination in many religious traditions around the world.[6,7] Native to India, the movement of peacocks around the world, both as symbols and the animals themselves, attests to the extraordinarily rich interrelationships of artistic cultures around the world and throughout time.

ID #20 1 2 3

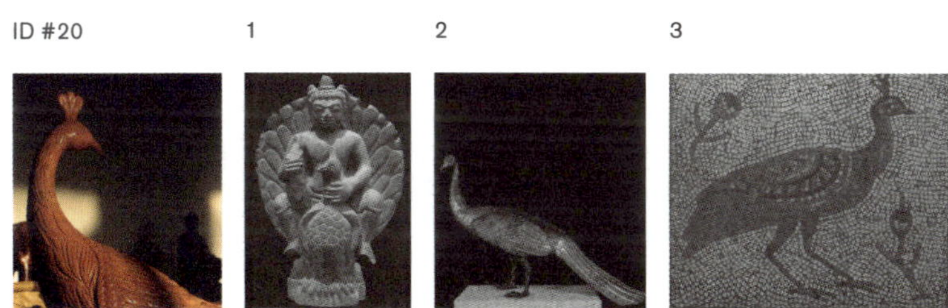

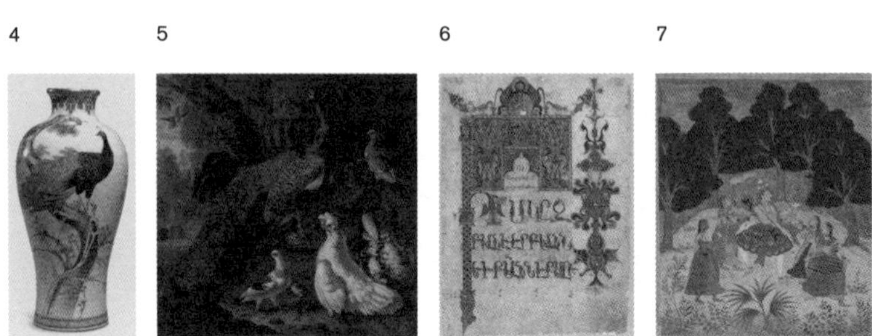

ID #21

GRIFFIN

With the body of a lion and the head and wings of an eagle, the griffin is perhaps one of the oldest and longest standing artistic symbols. Its presence in the iconographic record stretches in time and space from Ancient Egypt and the Pre-Iranian civilization of Elam in the late 4th millennium BCE, to Syria in the 2nd millennium BCE, after which it was ubiquitous throughout the Ancient Near East, spreading to Ancient Greece in what scholars call the "Orientalizing period" around the 7th century BCE, then to the Romans with whom it became especially popular in Imperial iconography, emerging again in the Christian iconography and heraldry of Medieval Europe, where it survived into the European Renaissance, and up through the 19th and even 20th and 21st centuries where it operates as a revivalist motif, or in more modernized forms as part of corporate brand identities. The written historical record does not attest to the cultural meaning of the griffin until the middle of the 5th centry BCE when the poetry of Arsiteas was first recorded in Greek. Later in the 1st century CE the griffin appears in Pliny the Elder's *Naturalis Historia*. In these accounts, the griffin is said to be a ferocious guardian of gold mines. These basic characteristics have remained throughout the many transformations in its cultural meanings: a fierce protector of value whether it be moral or mundane. The motif of the seated griffin with vertically extended front legs dates back to at least the Ancient Greek iconographic tradition.[1] As high relief architectural ornament it can be seen in Ancient Roman trapezophoros, or table supports. But the starkly upright orientation of the *Baragouin Griffin* with its especially compact footprint, sculpted fully in the round is most similar to British heraldic statuary,[2] which would typically be seen displaying a coat of arms near the front entrances or in the gardens of aristocratic residences.

ID #21 | 1 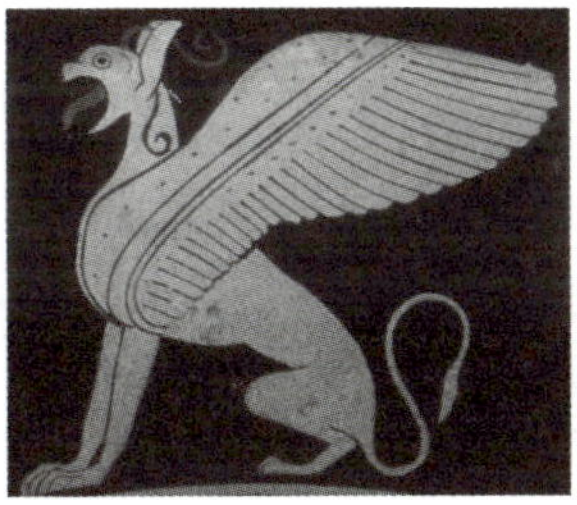 | 2

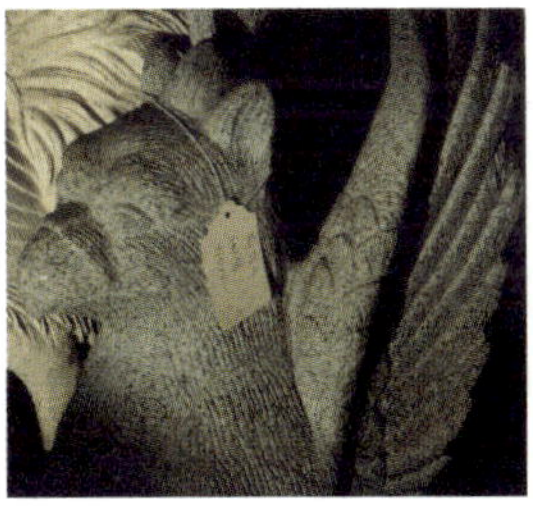

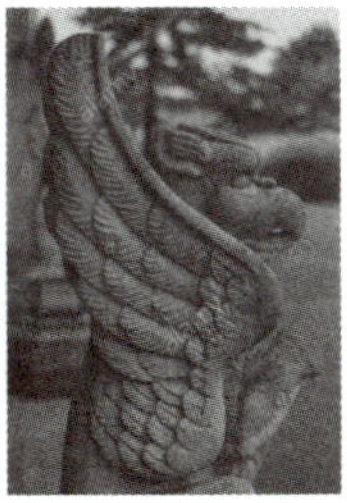

ID #22

SEATED DANAID

Ancient Greek mythology associated local springs with divine nymphs, goddesses of fertility, marriage and birth. Ancient depictions of nymphs typically feature urns from which they carried or poured water. One can see the revival of these themes throughout the Renaissance and later in Europe well into the 19th century; examples by John Thomas at the Kensington Gardens offer some loose prototypes for the *Baragouin* figure. But the downturned head and centrality of the pose is strongly reminiscent of a widely reproduced image by Pre-Raphaelite John William Waterhouse, *The Danaides* (1903). See ID #8 on the myth of the Danaides. Danaides have been popular figures in garden statuary, particularly for fountains because they are always portrayed carrying or pouring water from urns. The most commonly copied Danaid statue is an early 19th-century marble by Christian Daniel Rauch (1777–1857), which is now in the Hermitage Museum.[1] The major surviving ancient classical prototype of a Danaide is in the Vatican Museum.[2]

ID #22 1 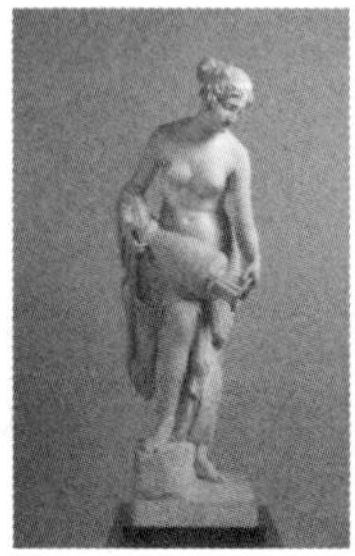 2

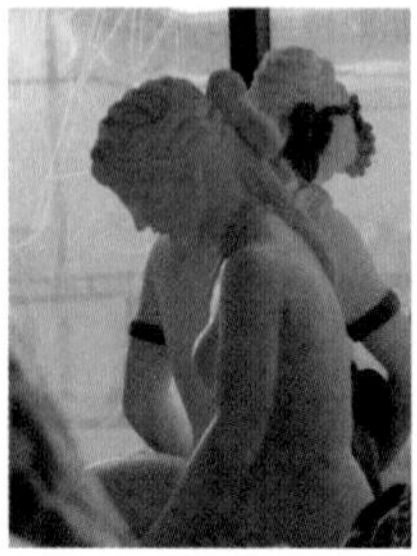

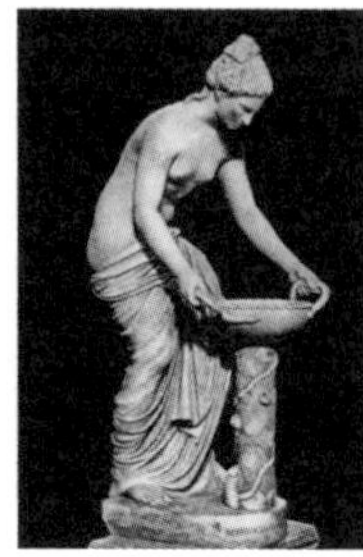

ID #23

WOMAN WITH BIRDS

This is a typical motif of 19th-century French Academic art: a young woman in Renaissance period costume with birds to signify her innocence. It also overlaps to some extent with the sensibilities of the Pre-Raphaelites in London, though these would have been less heavy handed with the Italianate influence in the costume. One finds prototypes in 19th century French academic sculptors such as *Woman with Birds* by Jean-Louis Gregoire (1840–1890),[1] or similarly *Young Woman with Birds* by Auguste Louis Mathurin Moreau (1834–1917).[2] The *Baragouin* example is notable for its marked classicism in comparison to the coy sentimentalism of these earlier French examples. Indeed, the pose of the *Baragouin Woman with Birds* is more like a less dynamic version of the *Callipygian Venus*,[3] a 1st-century BCE Roman marble statue, which was rediscovered in Italy in the 16th century. Ironically, the features that make the Callipygian Venus more dynamic, such as the raised left arm and the head twisted all the way around to peer at her backside (from whence derives the name: *kallypugos*, which is Greek for beautiful buttocks), are precisely those which were added by restorers in the 16th century, making the *Baragouin* statue an accidental after-image of the ancient original. Of course, to entertain this idea, one would have to ignore the birds.

ID #23 1 2 3

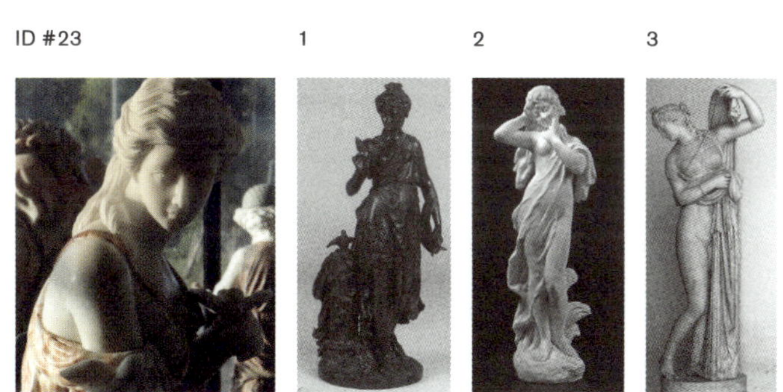

ID #24 WOMAN WITH FLOWERS

This figure is likely inspired by the Pre-Raphaelites' fascination with depicting young women in long flowing dresses with flowers in their hair. Shakespeare's Ophelia was a favored subject, but Greek myths were considered an equally appropriate armature for these kinds of pictures. One might think in particular of the work of John William Waterhouse, who featured flower sniffing, flower picking, flower bouquets, and other flowery accoutrements on young Shakespearean nymphs with unflinching regularity in his practice.[1] There is no specific prototype worth pointing to for the *Baragouin* example, especially given how rare sculptors are among the Pre-Raphaelites. Thomas Woolner (1825–1892) was the only sculptor among the founding members of the Pre-Raphaelite Brotherhood, and his sculpture, *Love* (1850s),[2] his only extant work depicting a standing woman, is similar to the *Baragouin* figure only in the requisite floral head gear, and perhaps in the starkly elongated bridge of the nose. It is otherwise remarkably classicizing for a Pre-Raphaelite work. This is perhaps not so surprising as it would seem that his status as a sculptor and his faltering art career estranged him from the group rather quickly. Indeed he spent a good bit of the 1850s as a gold-miner in Australia (also a failed venture), but found on his return to London in 1857 that the *Love* sculpture had earned him a strong reputation in his absence, whereupon he took up a successful run doing bust and full standing portraiture for a number of august institutions in and around London. There is an Ophelia statuette produced late in his career, but she is seated and not particularly florid. The *Baragouin* figure is thus better described as deriving from a Pre-Raphaelite style of painting, which has been adapted to sculptural form. The peculiar two-tone effect produced by the addition of a salmon/coral color to the dress and flowers is a uniquely contemporary flourish.

ID #24

1

2

ID #25

LIONS (OUTDOOR)

See ID #3 for a discussion of the Medici lions and other related sculptures, which are most closely related to the *Baragouin Lions*. Here, the rose marble material of the lions is quite unusual. It recalls the famous Verona Marble, which has long been a signal of the magnificence of Venetian splendor. Though they are significantly different in style from the *Baragouin* examples, lions sculpted in Verona Marble by Giovanni Bonazza (1654–1736) guard the entrance to Saint Mark's Basilica in Venice.[1] Another notable example of lions sculpted in Verona Marble can be seen at the entrance to Santa Maria Maggiore in Bergamo.[2]

ID #25

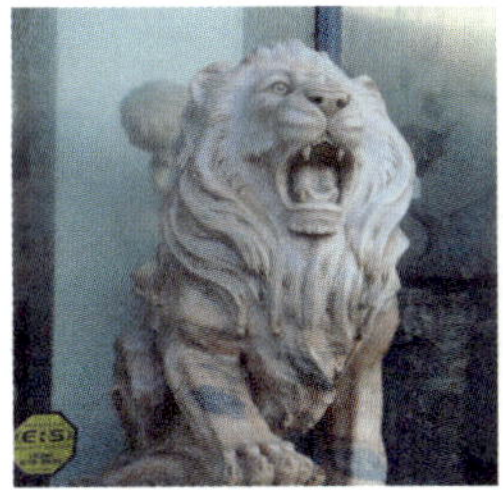

1

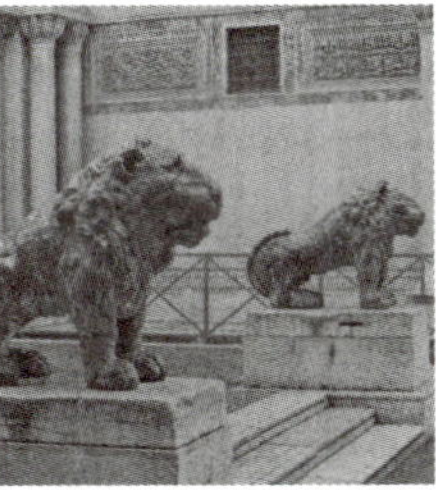

2

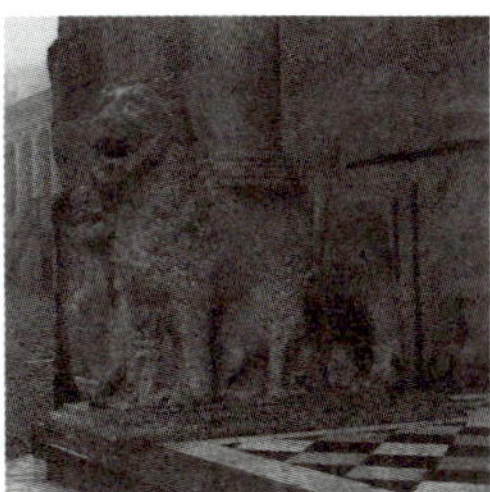

ID #26

ABSTRACT UNDRESS

Undress becomes an acceptable theme in the European tradition in early 18th-century French genre painting, beginning with *A Lady at her Toilet* (1717–1719) by Antoine Watteau (1684–1721), now in the Wallace Collection in London.[1] Rarely do we find such a literal depiction of the gesture of undressing, even after the theme of the toilette is taken up as an acceptable subject for a genre painting. Jean-Honoré Fragonard (1732–1806) would reprise Watteau's composition in the 1770s,[2] but the Watteau is remarkable for the posture of the figure, the woman's upraised arms and exposed breasts, combined with the starkness of her gaze, which is neither coy nor demure. The *Baragouin* figure borrows from this posture, but in the place of the upper half of her face, as well as the remainder of the figure above the shoulders and below the hips, we are confronted with a completely different topos, that of the non finito, introduced into the modern canon of Western sculpture by Donatello (1386–1466), but most remembered in the work of Michelangelo (1475–1564) whose *Slaves*[3] and *Atlas* (1530s), now at the Accademia Gallery in Florence, remain a staple of art historical interpretation. They are some of the earliest examples of the conflated dramatization of the subject matter of a work and the work of the artist with their materials, one of the pillars of the modern fascination with the hand of the artist. Of course, the non-finito parts of the *Baragouin* example are actually roughly but evenly finished with a distinctly mechanical horizontal stripe pattern, which gives the work a strangely industrial aura, referencing Brutalist architectural surfaces, as with Paul Rudolph's Rudolph Hall from 1963 in Boston.[4] Contemporary examples of this posture are most common in pin-up art and photography.[5]

ID #26

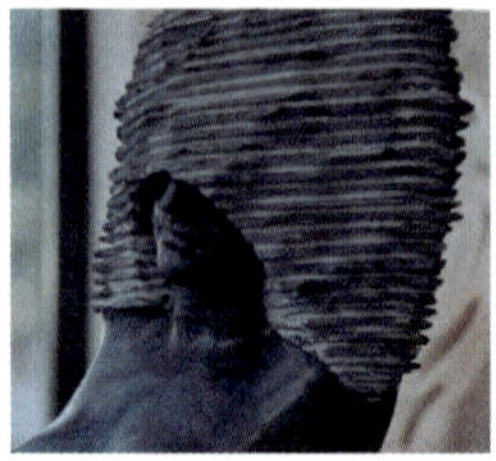

1

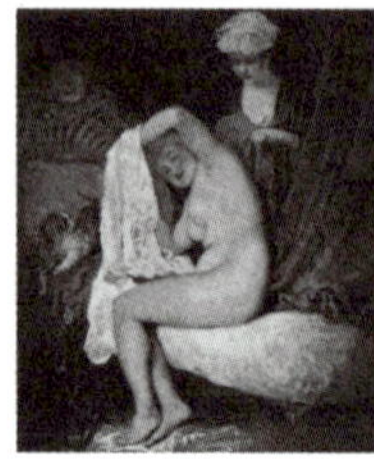

2

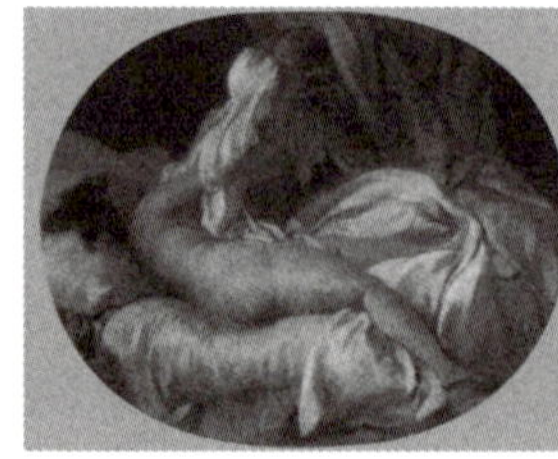

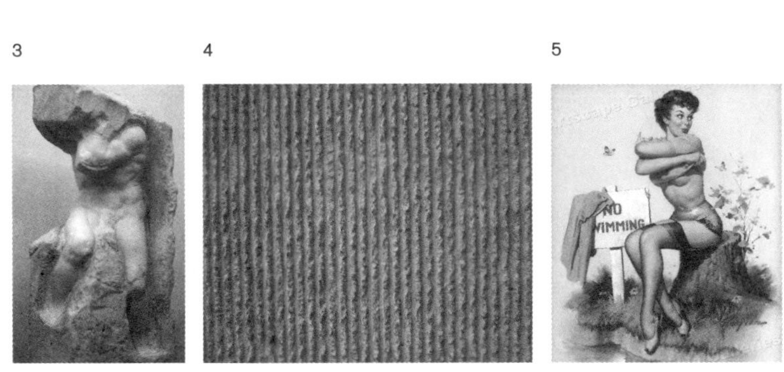
3
4
5

ID #27

THE EMBRACE

This is another sculpture that partakes in a kind of blunted sentimentalization of the mid-20th-century biomorphic abstraction pioneered by artists such as Jean (Hans) Arp (1886–1966), Henry Moore (1898–1986), Barbara Hepworth (1903–1975), etc. One thinks especially in this case of Hepworth's *Mother and Child* sculpture of 1934, now at the Wakefield Art Gallery in Wakefield UK,[1] as well as the more horizontally oriented sculpture of the same title and year now at the Tate in London,[2] because of the emphasis on paired interlocking figures, but the shape of the figures is something modeled more closely from Arp's 1961 *Déméter*, carved in marble, which recently sold at Christies for 5.8 million dollars—more than doubling the opening price. Arp also cast an edition of five in bronze four years later.[3] Most of the bronze casts are in private collections, though several have appeared on the auction market in the last decade.

ID #27 1 2 3

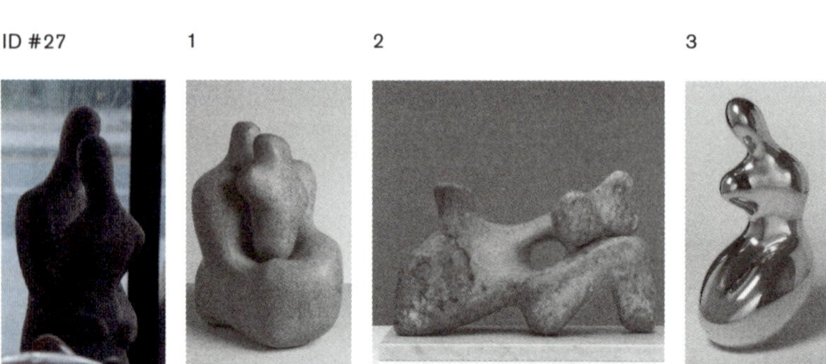

ID #28 APHRODITE ANADYOMENE

The shape of the hips, belly, and bust of this figure strongly suggest a classical prototype. The only Aphrodite/Venus characteristically depicted with her arms raised is Aphrodite Anadyomene, who is most often depicted with hands raised holding her hair off of her shoulders. An ancient bronze example is in the Musée Royal de Mariemont.[1] This is said to be the moment that she fixes her hair after emerging from the sea foam, hence the name Anadyomene, meaning rising up. In the *Baragouin* version, the hair has been replaced by a garland of roses, a flower which often served as an attribute of Aphrodite, though the garland recalls 18th-century adaptations such as Antonio Canova's (1757–1822) *Dancer with Finger on Chin* (1819/1823), now at the National Gallery of Art in Washington, D.C.,[2] as well as in similar variations of the Pre-Raphaelites (see ID #25).

ID #28

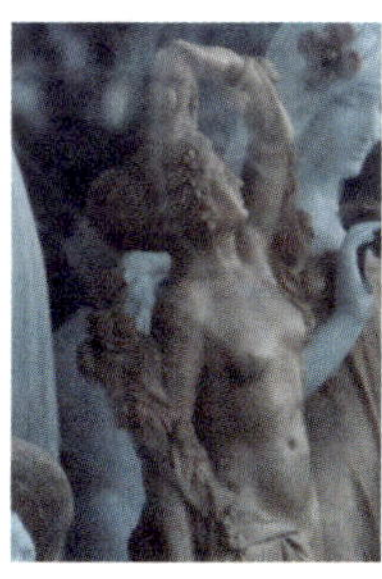

1

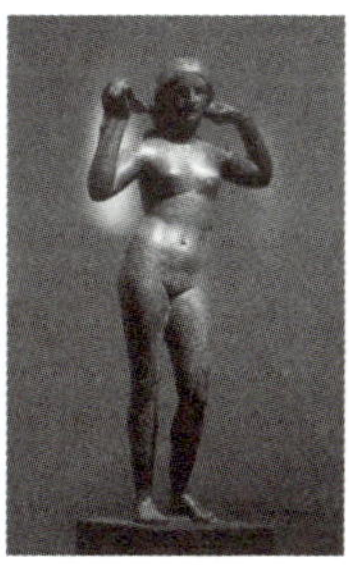

2

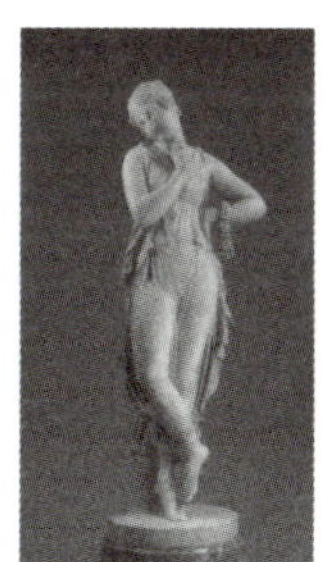

ID #29

CRANE

The crane is a ubiquitous subject of Chinese and Japanese pictorial art. It is less often represented in statuary, but iconic examples in cast bronze can be found in China in the Forbidden City[1] and in the Imperial Summer Palace. During the Meiji era In Japan, a strong market for cast bronze crane statues emerged, many of these were exported to Europe,[2] where they were commonly used as garden ornaments. The crane is a symbol of grace and longevity in many cultures throughout the world. One also finds crane dances in many different cultural contexts, no doubt, inspired by the crane's elaborate mating rituals. In Greek mythology, the crane dance is associated with the cult of Theseus. In the tradition of the Ainu, the indigenous peoples of Hokkaido, Japan, the crane dance is a show of respect and gratitude to the spirits. It is still performed regularly, and has recently been recognized on the UNESCO Lists of Intangible Cultural Heritage. It was famously captured on film for the first time in 1908 when photographer Arnold Genthe visited the Ainu people. The photographs from his visit are available in the United States Library of Congress, as well as in the Allen Memorial Art Museum at Oberlin College.[3]

ID #29 1 2 3

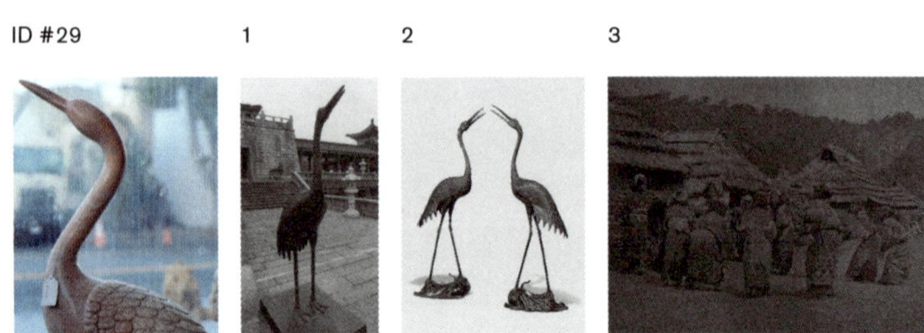

ID #30

FU DOGS

"Fu dogs" or "fu lions" are European names for these ancient Chinese lion sculptures, which in China are typically referred to as stone lions (石獅; Shíshī) or bronze lions (銅獅; Tóngshī) depending on the material in which they are shaped; stone being the older and by far the more common material. Stone lions date back to the Han Dynasty (206 BCE–220 CE), and have maintained their symbolic meanings and fundamental iconographic vocabulary since this time. They are typically displayed in pairs on either side of an entrance way. The one on the left representing the Yin, or female, energy is portrayed with a cub playing under one front paw,[1] and the one on the right representing Yang, or male, energy is portrayed with one front paw on an embroidered ball.[2] Stone lions act as guardian spirits, nurturing and protecting those inside of the structure that they guard.

ID #30

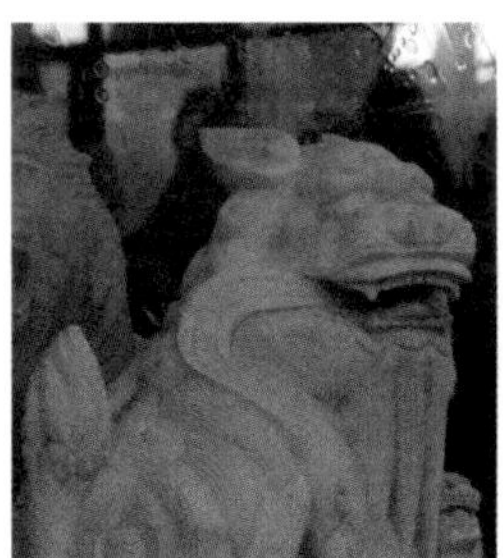

1

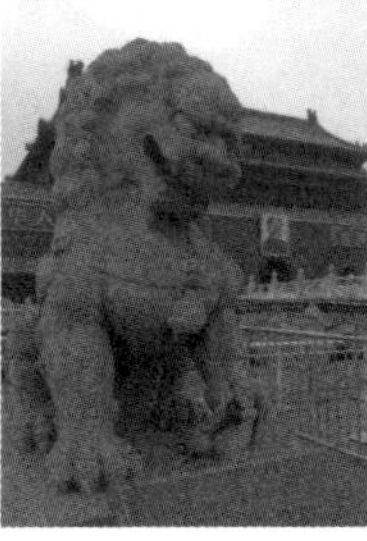

2

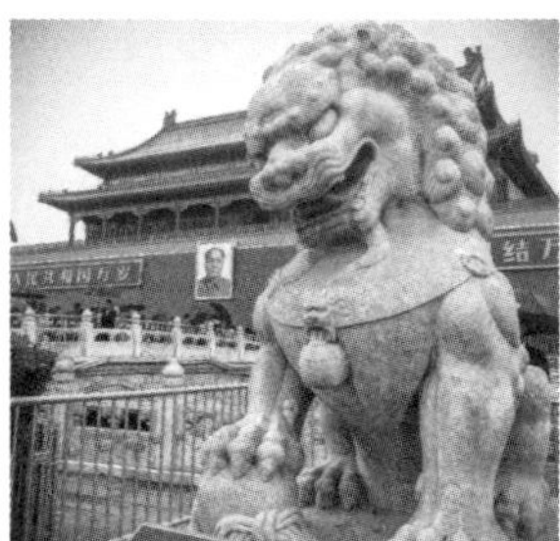

ID #31

THE RING

This is a widely repeated motif in the wedding chapel industry.[1] Something about the scale of this work recalls the public sculptures of Claes Oldenburg and Coosje van Bruggen representing oversized everyday objects, such as *Mistos (Match Cover)* (1989) in Barcelona and *Saw, Sawing* (1996) in Tokyo.[2] Perhaps it is simply that these works always call to mind a giant unseen hand about to make use of them, but one also thinks of the general tendency of Oldenburg and van Bruggen to inflict their characteristic scale shifting operation on what seem to be cartoon drawings of objects rather than actual objects, an effect which is visible in the *Baragouin* sculpture in the lack of detail in the hands, but doubly emphasized by the peculiarly disjointed combination of the literal forms of the hands and ring balanced on the ideal form of a the semi-toroidal heart.

This sculptural form is also on display in Stepanakert, Armenia,[3] the capital of the self-declared independent Nagorno-Karabakh Republic. Colloquially known as the "Hands" statue, it sits in front of the Alley of Lovers leading up to the Presidential Palace, which features a staircase flanked by lamps with their posts sculpted to resemble brides and a bridegrooms.

ID #31

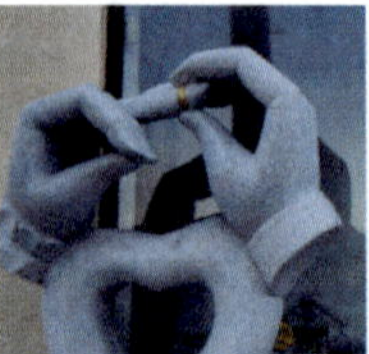

1

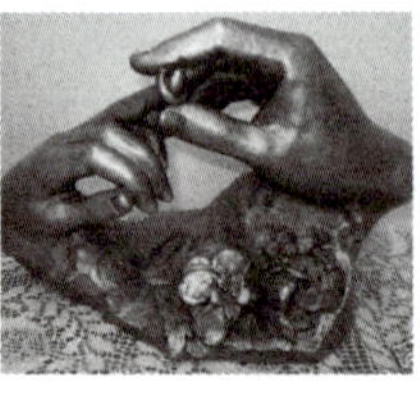

2

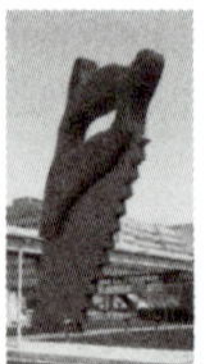

3

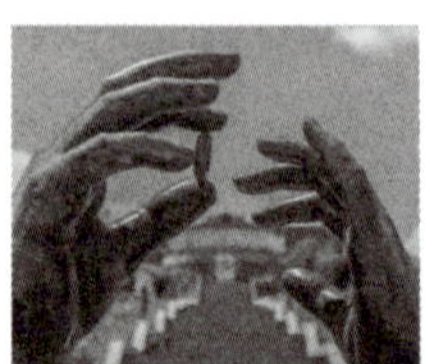

ID #32

DUTCH BOY

The hat and the hair, and the tilt of the head are strongly reminiscent of Frans Hals' *Young Man and Woman in an Inn* (1623) now at the Metropolitan museum in New York.[1] But the tone is completely different. The Hals has a bawdiness that is altogether lacking in the *Baragouin* depiction, which feels more innocent, something closer to Rembrandt's *Portrait of a Boy* (1655–60), now at the Norton Simon Museum in Pasadena,[2] or like a French Rococo reinterpretation of the Baroque Dutch boy image filtered through the trope of the innocent shepherd, which was so common in popular French theater of the early 18th century.[3] And perhaps also reimagined, finally, as the packaging for a 19th-century American bar of soap, designed to fend off the swelling popularity of the young maiden featured in the advertising of the French soap brand Savon de Marseille.[4]

ID #32 | 1 | 2 | 3 | 4

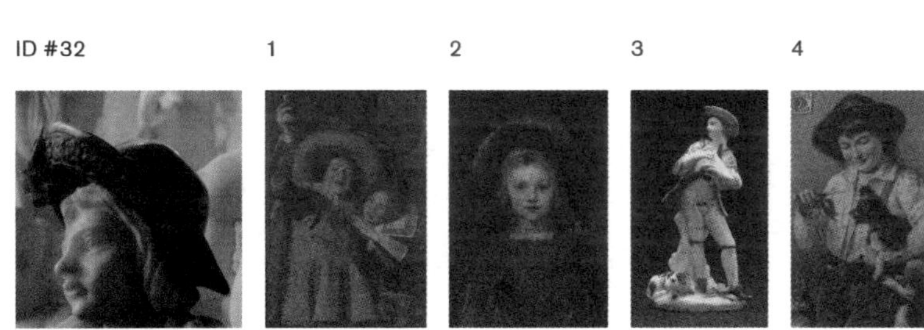

ID #33

ALLEGORICAL FIGURE

Although there is not enough visible detail to securely identify this figure, the strongly classicized influence of Roman statuary suggests that she is an allegorical figure. The position of her arms, one reaching across the body and both hands resting on what appears to be a long handle or shaft, recalls the figure of Amphitrite, wife of Poseidon and eldest of the 50 Nereids. One strong precedent, particularly notable for the stoic classicism of the posture and facial expression, is *Amphitrite with downturned trident* (1866), by François Théodore Devaulx (1808–1870), now in the north façade of the Cour Carrée in the Louvre palace, Paris.[1] A more dynamic example by Léon François Chervet (1834–1900) is now in the Place de la Marine in Agde, France.[2] This version was originally displayed without her allegorical association on the façade of the Palais du Trocadéro, Paris, built for the Exposition Universelle (1878), which was demolished to make way for the Exposition of 1937. The seated posture of the *Baragouin* example, with one foot slightly elevated as though resting on a step, is not common in depictions of Amphitrite, but one sees it in other classicized ornamental figures, such as the allegorical figure of the Neva river[3] on Vasilievsky spit island in Saint Petersburg, Russia.

ID #33 1 2 3

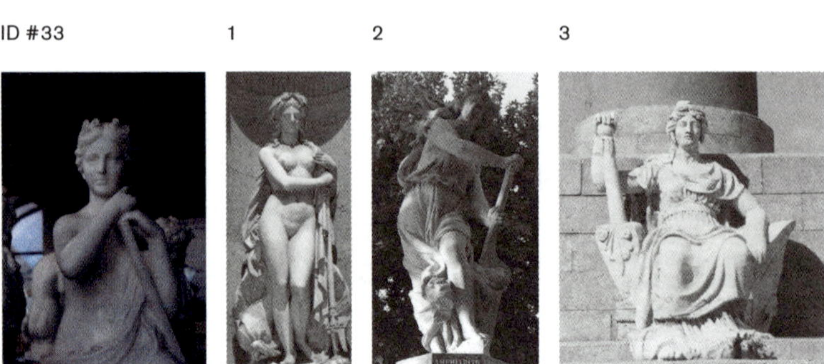

ID #34

FUHU LUOHAN

Fuhu Luohan, also known as Pindola in Sanskrit, and Binzuru in Japanese, is the 18th Arhat (Luohan) in Chinese Mahayana Buddhism. He is known as the tiger-taming Arhat. Arhats represent the original disciples of the Buddha, charged with protecting the dharma in the earthly realm. Their statues ornament Buddhist temples.

Representations of the Luohan have existed in Chinese Buddhist art since at least the 5th century. During the 10th century in China, the conventional 16 Arhat of the Indian tradition were expanded to 18, and became popular subjects in both painting and sculpture. The most famous painter of the Luohans was a monk named Guanxiu. It is said that they appeared to him in a dream, and he subsequently painted their portraits. Each was briefly eulogized by the Qianlong Emperor in the 18th century. Fuhu Luohan's eulogy is translated as follows:

> Precious ring with magical powers,
> Infinitely resourceful.
> Vigorous and powerful,
> Subduing a ferocious tiger.

It is usually accompanied by the following explanation:

> Pindola was a Brahmin and a general. Because he was devoted to Buddhism, which forbids killing, he was ordered by the king to become a monk. He joined a monastery in the mountains where he could hear a tiger howling every day. He said that the tiger

---

ID #34

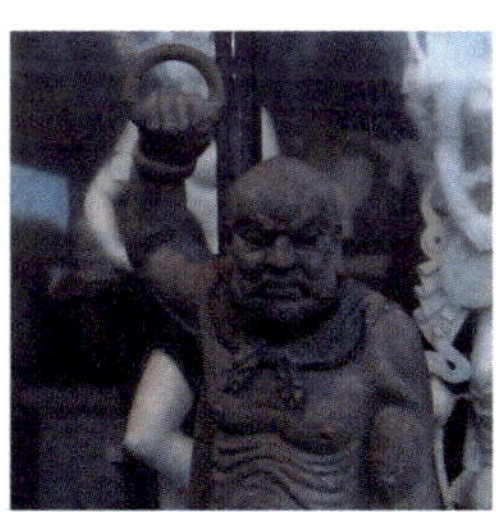

1

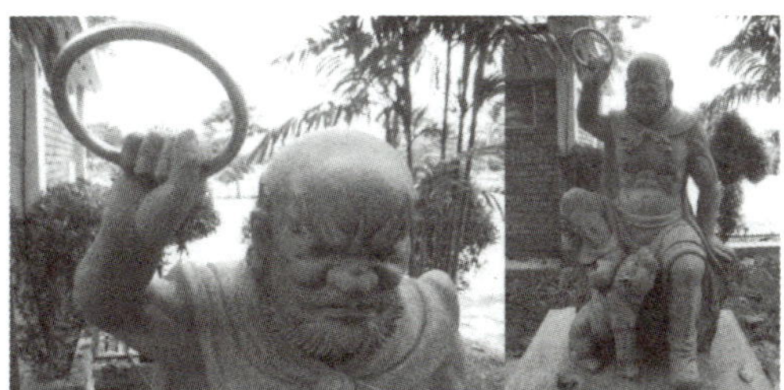

> was probably hungry and should be fed some vegetarian food. Otherwise the tiger might become a man-eater. So Pindola collected food from the monks and put it in a bucket which he left outside the monastery. The tiger did come for the food every night. After a period of time, the tiger was tamed. Thus Pindola was referred to as the Taming Tiger Arhat.

Fuhu Luohan is typically depicted holding a ring and subduing a tiger. An example very close to the *Baragouin* figure is on view in the garden of 18 Arhats at Pahang Buddhist Association Temple in Kuantan, Malaysia.[1] Typically, statues of the 18 Arhats stand guard in the main hall of a Buddhist temple.[2] A late 19th-century statuette with a very different bearing is in the collection of the National Gallery of Australia in Canberra.[3] Originally, the Luohan were depicted as unkempt foreigners with bushy eyebrows, long noses, facial hair, and often hairy hands and feet, but later depictions softened these features considerably. Ink rubbings made in the 18th century from stone steles said to have been carved based on Guanxiu's 10th century paintings reflect the early style.[4] The paintings are lost, making these ink rubbings some of the only surviving evidence of Guanxiu's style.

2 3 4

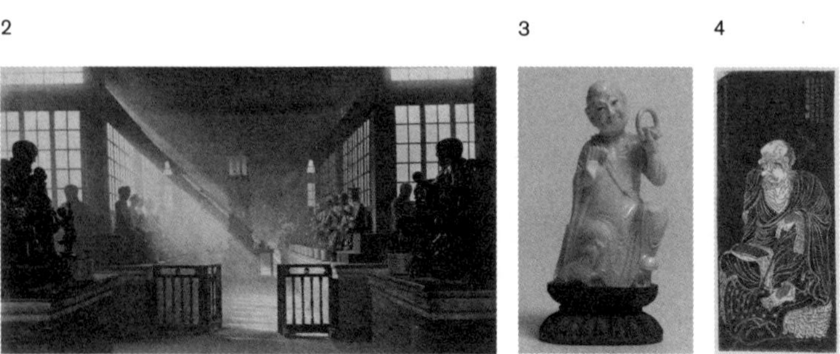

ID #35/36

WAGNERIANS

This is an especially bizarre set of figures, even in the already markedly idiosyncratic *Baragouin* context. Perhaps it is the distinct coloring on their various apparel—clothing, plumed hats, arm bands—set against the almost completely flat white of their exposed flesh, combined with their lithe and relatively neutral physique, which make these figures look more like a set of department store mannequins than statues. Admittedly, they achieve much more dynamic postures than would be possible with your average mannequin, but this seems to heighten the effect rather than diminish it, and even lends a strongly comic valence. Regarding their costumes, these are undoubtedly drawn from the repertoire of early Wagnerian productions at Bayreuth—the arm bands, the overzealous embossment of chest gear, even the feathers seem to draw on the winged helmets of the Valkyrie.[1,2] Although, one would also have to acknowledge the strong reference to the fashionable feathered bonnets of the early 1920s.[3]

ID #35/36 1 2 3

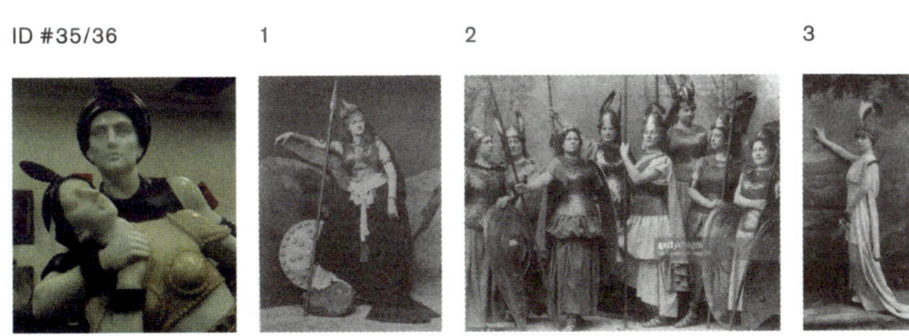

ID #37

GUAN YIN (COMPASSIONATE MOTHER)

This figure represents Guan Yin, the Buddhist figure of the Compassionate Mother (see ID #10). The elevated headdress, urna or baihao on the forehead, and long flowing robes are the primary identifying features. The figure presents the mudra of good fortune with her right hand by touching the thumb and ring finger.[1] In the other hand she is likely holding an unfurled scroll, which represents the Dharma, the teaching of the Buddha contained in the Buddhists texts known as the sutras.

ID #37

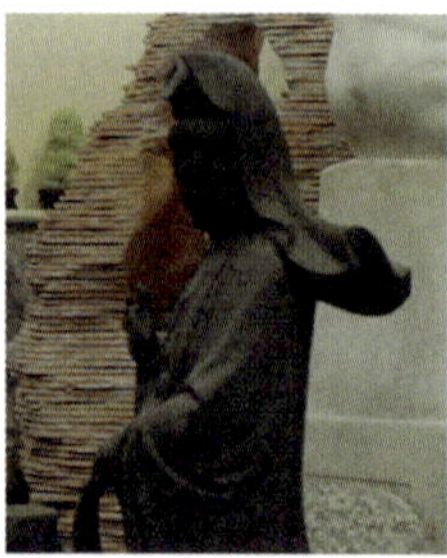

1

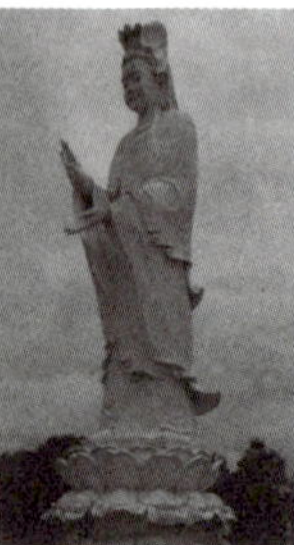

ID #38

DIE SCHAMHAFTIGKEIT (PUDEUR)

This is another version of the "modesty" theme taken from the Aphrodite of Knidos, exemplified in the Roman copy now known as the Capitoline Venus (see ID #11). Here the coy demeanor and raised pinky of the *Baragouin* figure recall Antonio Canova's (1757–1822) *Dancer with Finger on Chin* (1819/1823), now at the National Gallery of Art in Washington, D.C.[1] The modern treatment of the hair is reminiscent of the *Baragouin Temptation of Eve* (see ID #13), and the combination of references lends this figure a contemporary cast, as though we could imagine her in Fassbinder's *Lola*.[2]

ID #38

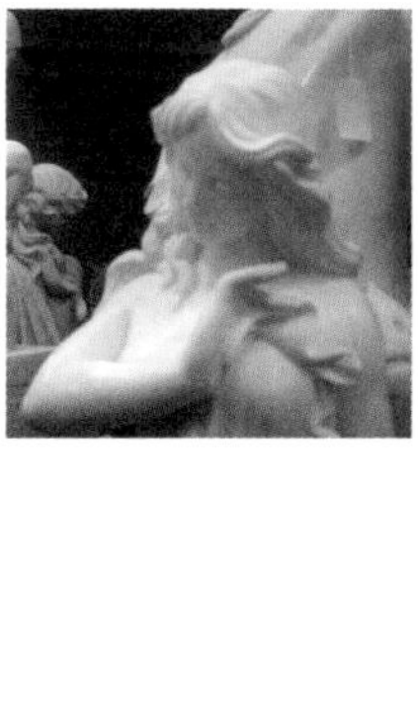

1

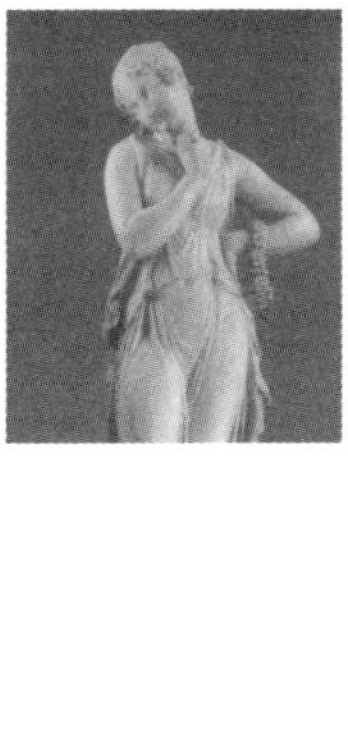

2

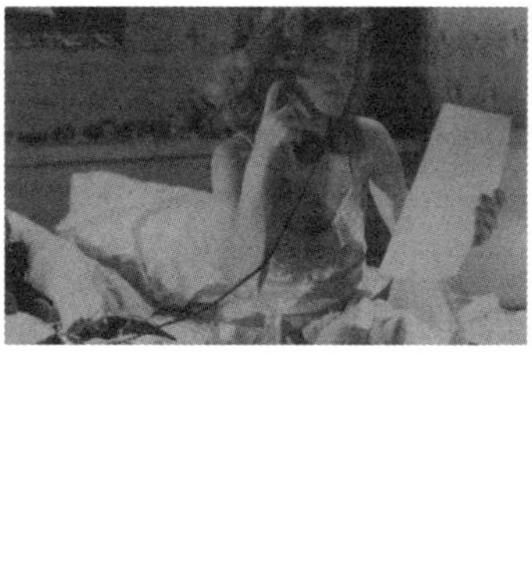

ID #39 NUDE FIELDING BIRDS

While there are no clear precedents for this figure, the conflation of classicized nude and romantic reinterpretation of pastoral and arcadian themes recalls the late work of the 19th-century British painter John Reinhard Weguelin (1849–1927). One thinks in particular of his 1878 work *Lesbia*, which brings bird feeding explicitly into the topos of the classical nude.[1] The thrown back head and lyrically expressive arms of the *Baragouin* nude give the effect of an almost ecstatic connection to the birds. The theme becomes a common place of conventional patriarchal fantasies conflating innocence and sensuality in the figure of a young woman communing with nature.[2,3,4,5]

ID #39 1 2

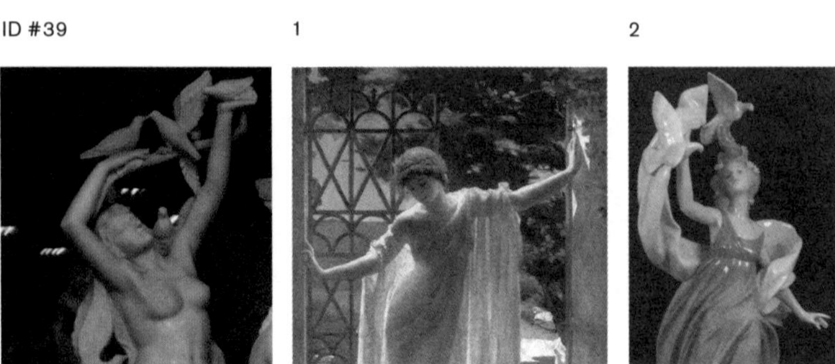

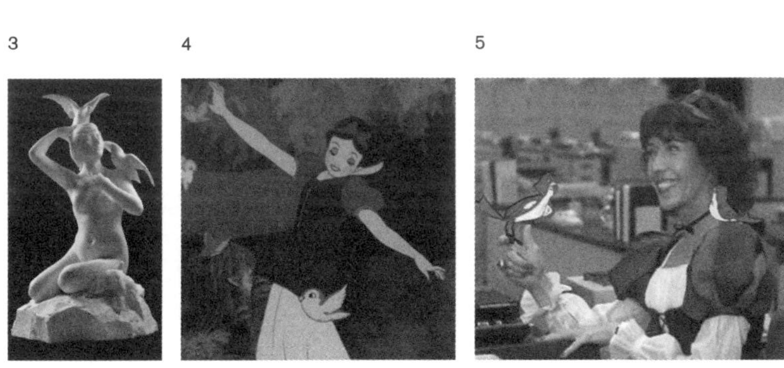

ID #40

ANGEL

Angels first appear widely in sculptural form as jamb sculptures for Gothic cathedrals, such as those which appear on the west facade of Reims Cathedral.[1] While these sculptures are not fully in the round, as is the *Baragouin Angel,* they do display the characteristically loose and manifold garments of High Gothic angel statuary, which carry over into later iconography. The *Baragouin Angel* is also notably distinct from these early predecessors in the solemn expression of her face and downturned head, which are common characteristics for angel statues in cemeteries. An example from the Ostfriedhof in Munich is particularly apt.[2]

ID #40 1 2

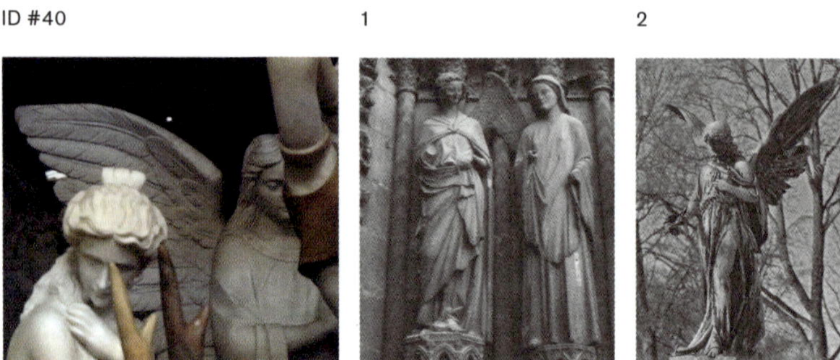

ID #41

WOMAN WITH WHEAT

Another allegorical figure in the *Baragouin* pantheon, here she holds a bundle of wheat, which symbolizes the abundance of the harvest. Typically associated with Ceres, Roman goddess of the harvest, this was a common subject of 19th-century decorative figurines.[1] One also sees this allegorical symbol represented frequently in public art throughout the midwestern United States, particularly in post offices and city halls.[2]

ID #41

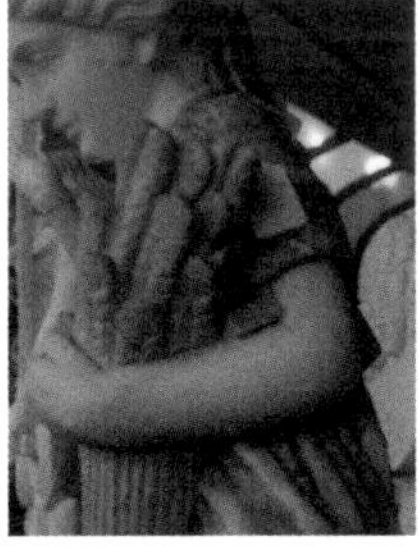

1

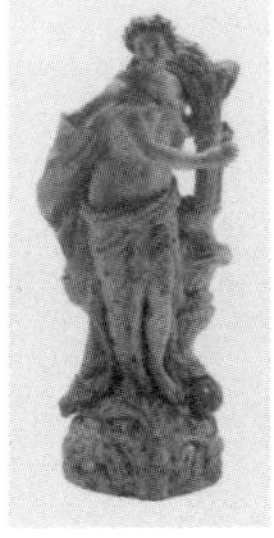

2

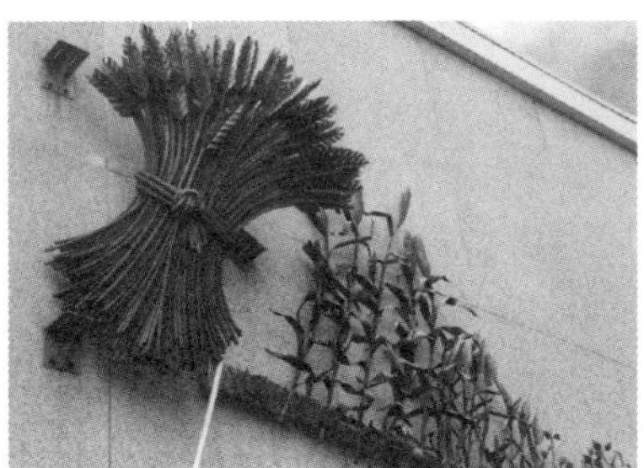

ID #42

BUST AFTER BACH

Although little can be seen of this figure, it is likely based on a portrait bust of the famed German composer Johann Sebastian Bach by German sculptor Carl Ludwig Seffner (1861–1932), which is now at the St. Thomas Church in Leipzig.[1] Bach busts are extremely prominent in the popular market for decorative sculpture. His iconic status as one of the great geniuses of the European musical tradition has made his bust one of the few that retains any of the traditional valence of bust statuary in a popular context. This kind of reverence sustains surprising relevance in the musical arts largely because the skill—not to say virtuosity—required to perform the works of the traditional canon are still hard won and highly prized. The de-skilling of most of the visual arts, by technological means, conceptual sophistication, and through the embrace of almost any medium have made irreverence the dominant sensibility in this field.

ID #42 1

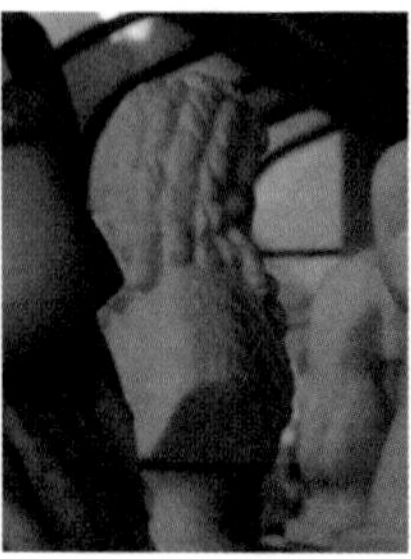

ID #43

LAUGHING BUDDHAS (SEATED)

The figure of Budai appears regularly in Buddhist temple art in China beginning in the Ming period, 1368–1644. Budai is named for his eternally plentiful cloth sack, which is one of his conventional attributes, along with his portly stature and cheerful disposition. He was adopted into the Chan Buddhist tradition in the mid-12th century as part of an effort to popularize Buddhism by incorporating heroes from folk traditions into the official pantheon. As a symbol of abundance, contentment, good humor, and happiness, Budai has been embraced by Buddhist traditions around Asia, including Japan, where he is known as Hotei, as well as Thailand, and Vietnam among others. The Wat Plai Laem Buddhist temple compound on Samui's northeast coast in Thailand houses a particularly striking example of a monumental scale version of this figure.[1] But perhaps more interesting is how ubiquitous Budai is as a popular devotional figure, so much so that his folkloric roots seem to have resurfaced as a dominant aspect despite his Ming period adoption into the Chan pantheon. Budai figures began to circulate widely in the late 16th century as part of the global porcelain trade, and in the west, they have often been mistakenly taken to be statues of the Buddha.

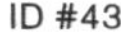
ID #43

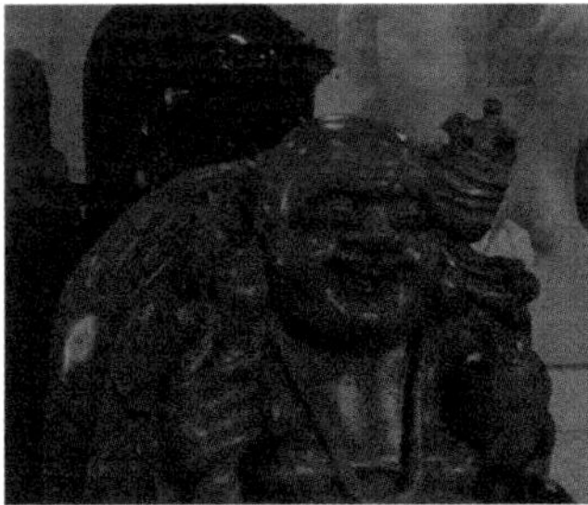

1

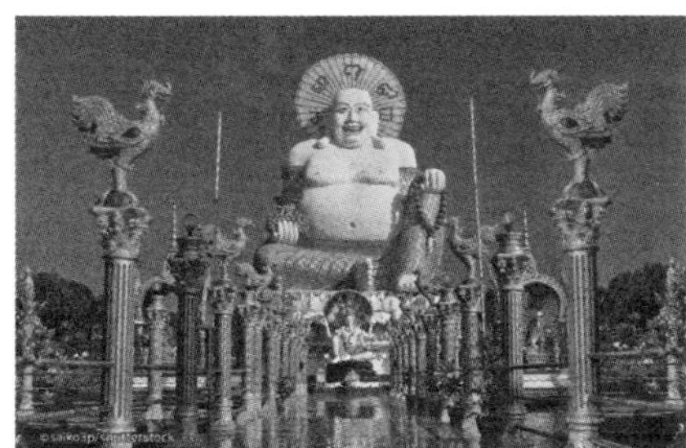

"Oooh!
Pierce his border
or beak
(Oooh! like this!"
Pierce his
border or
beak
like this!)

—WOMAN WITH WHEAT
ID #41

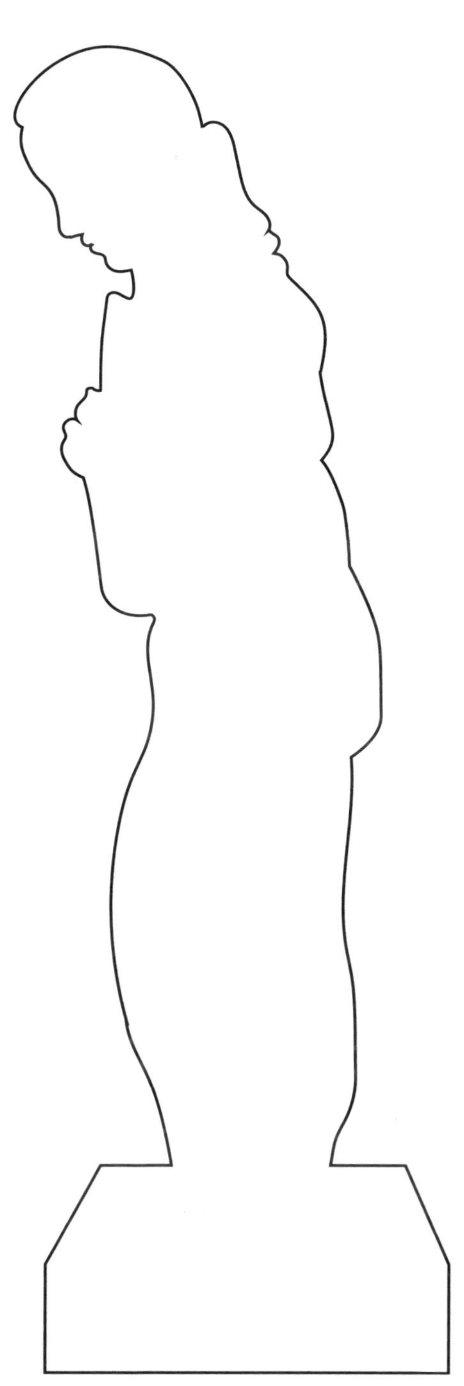

BARAGOUIN
VIDEO STILLS

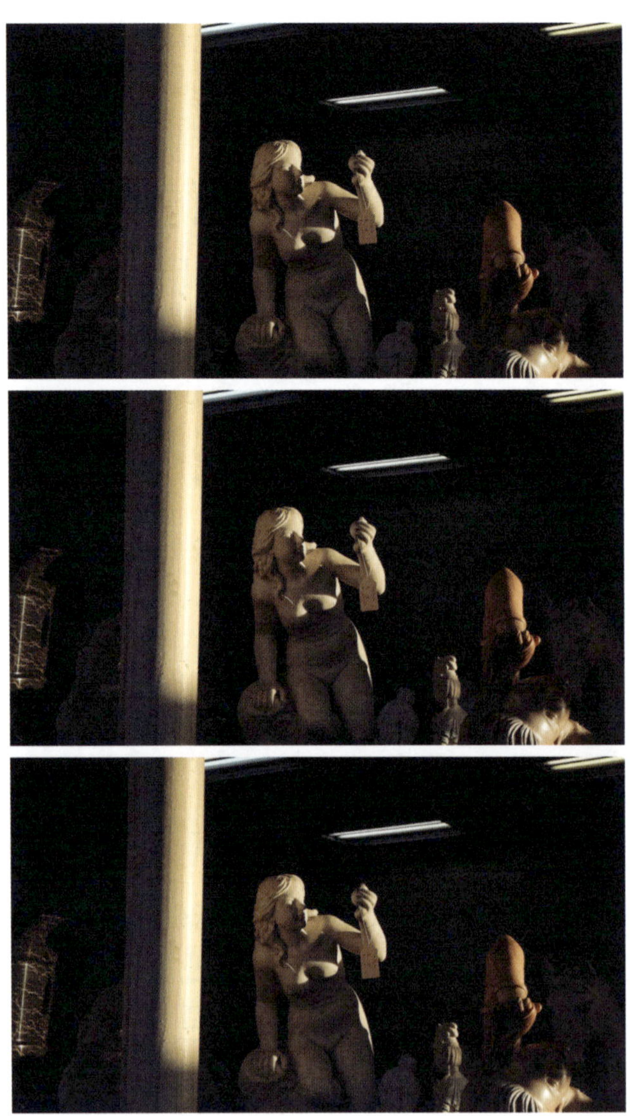

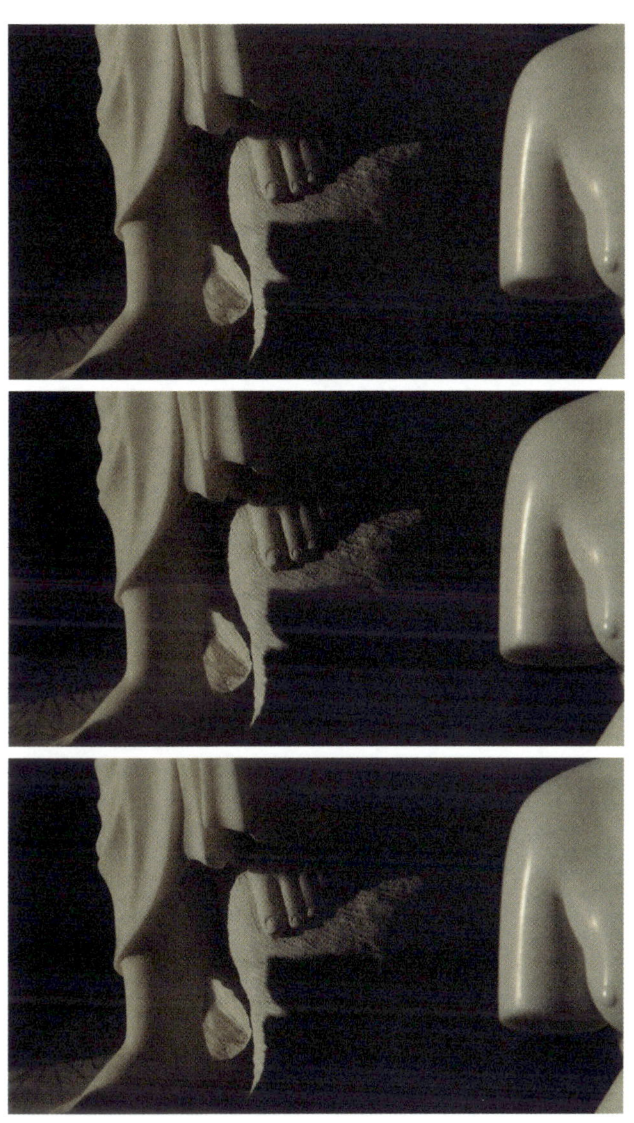

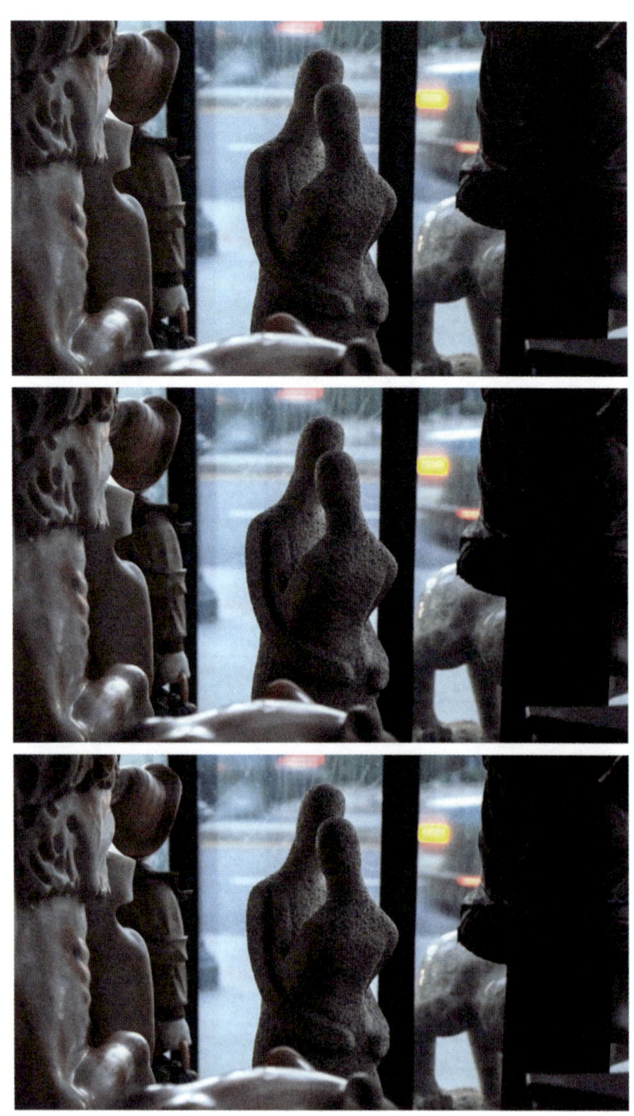

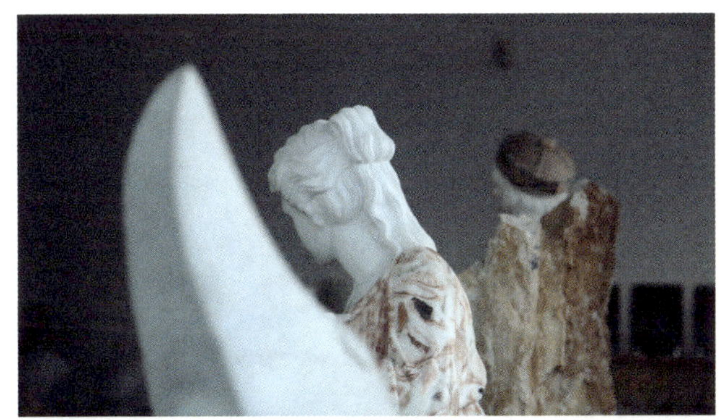

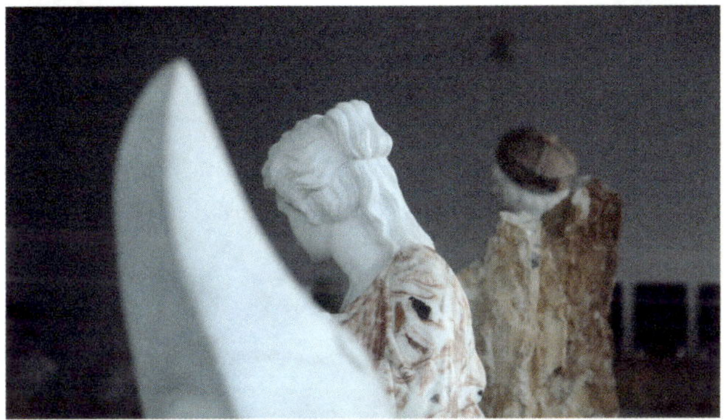

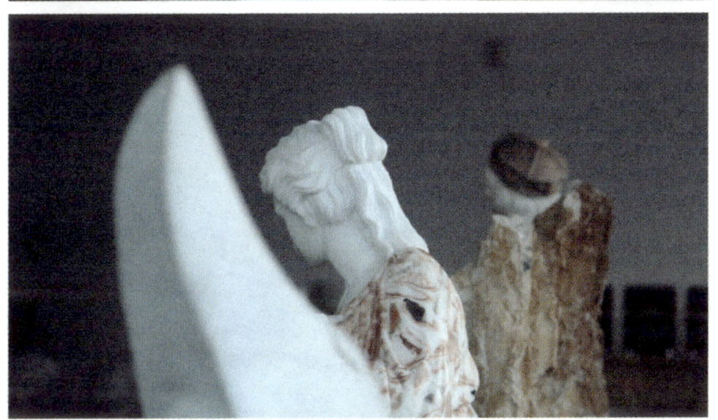

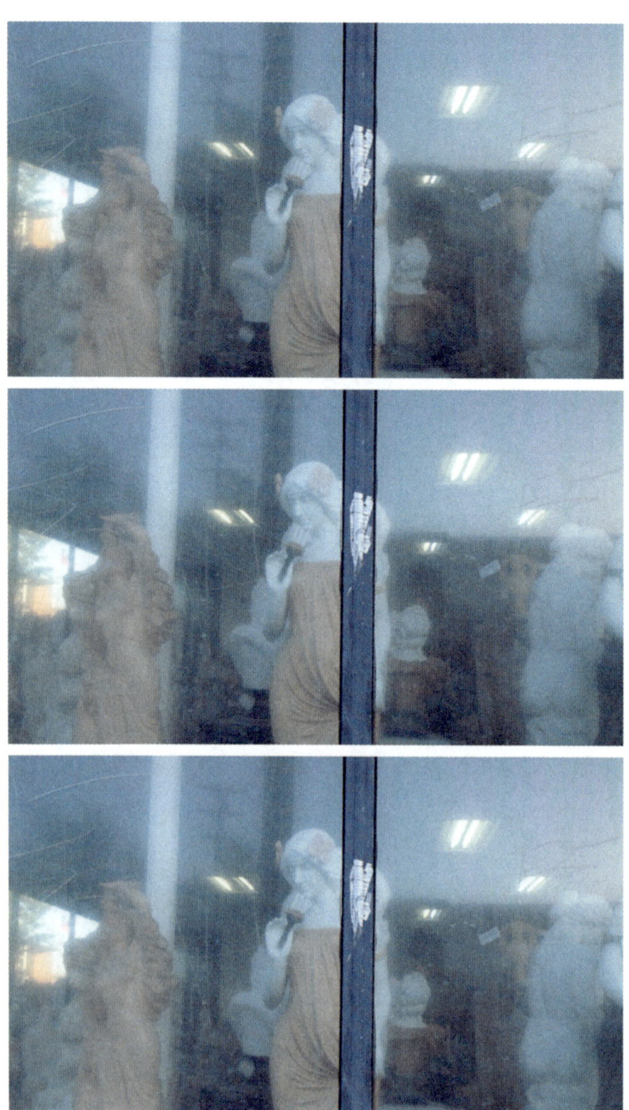

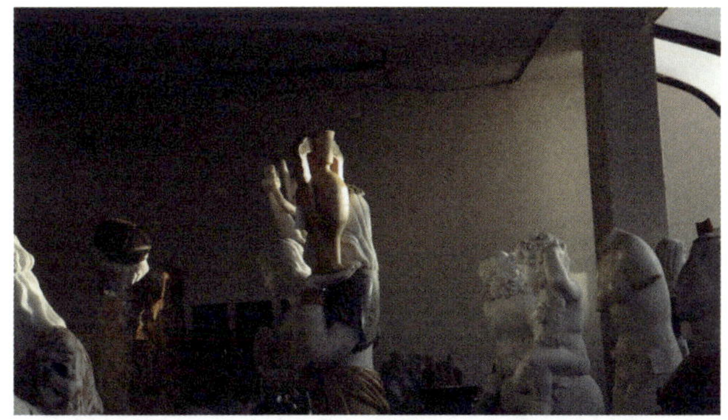

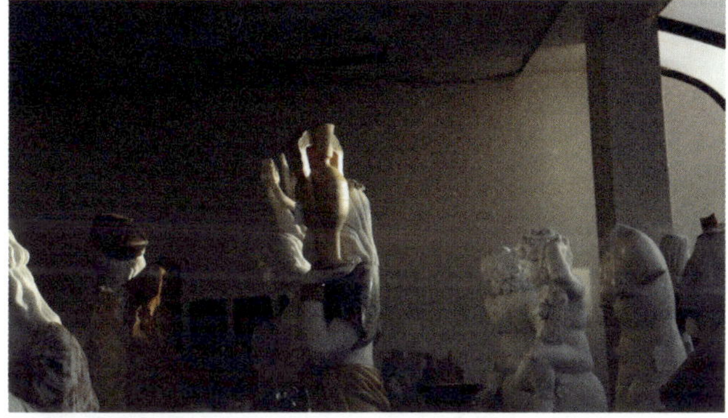

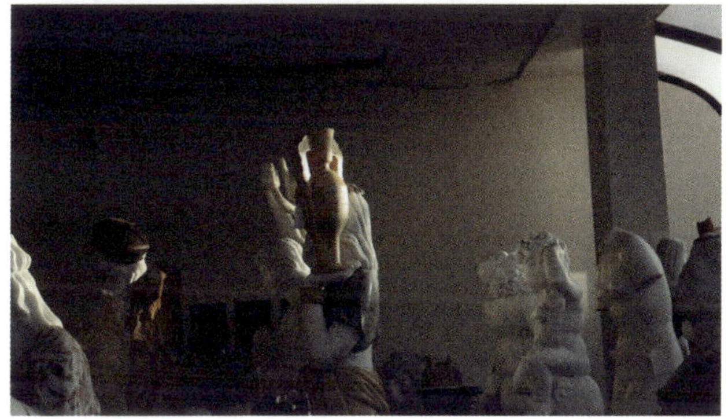

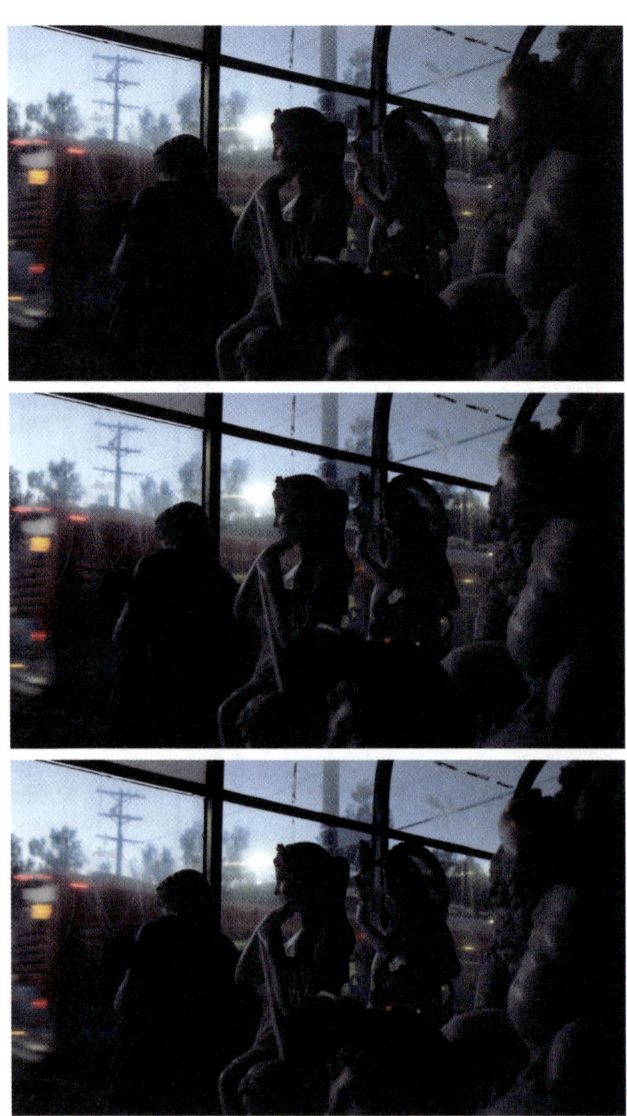

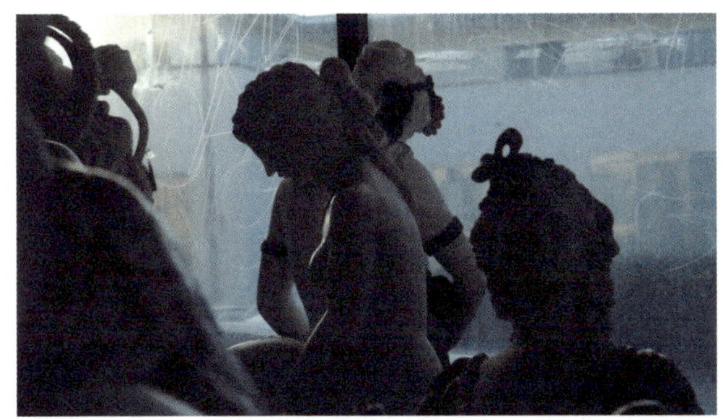

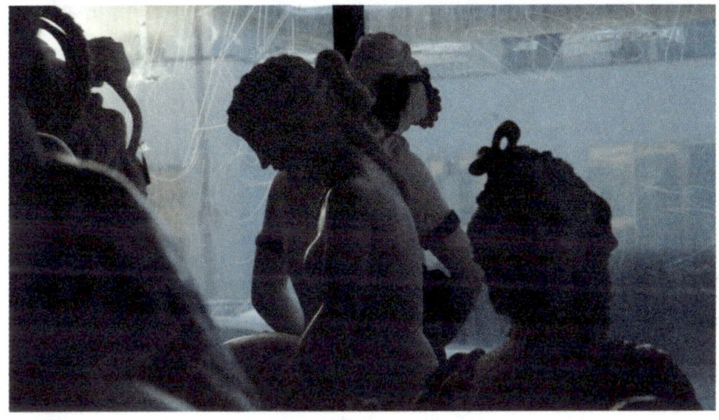

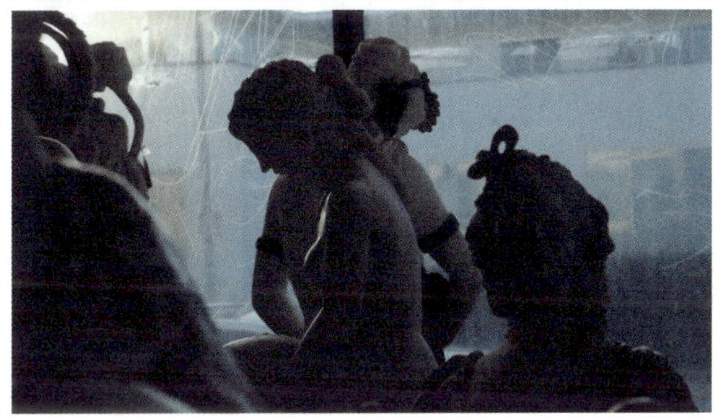

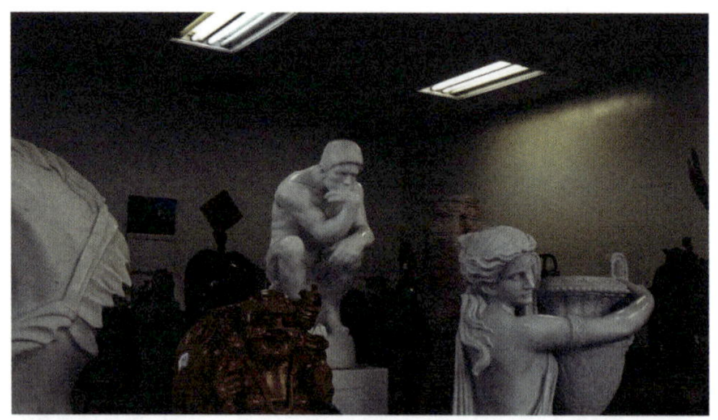

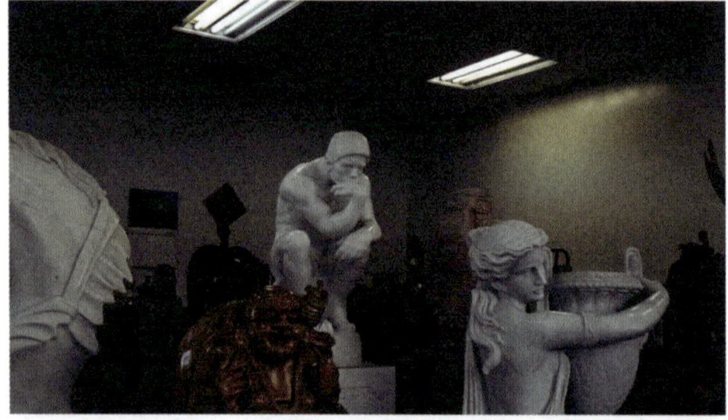

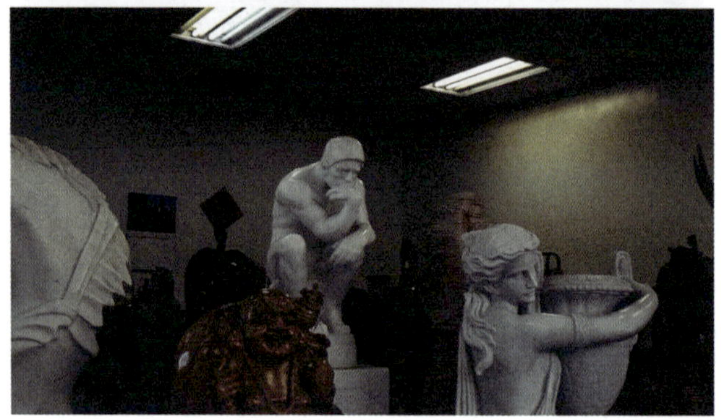

ALL VIDEO STILLS (PAGES 66–77):
Baragouin
Single-channel video (color, added sound)
with five-channel audio
10 min 04 sec
2021

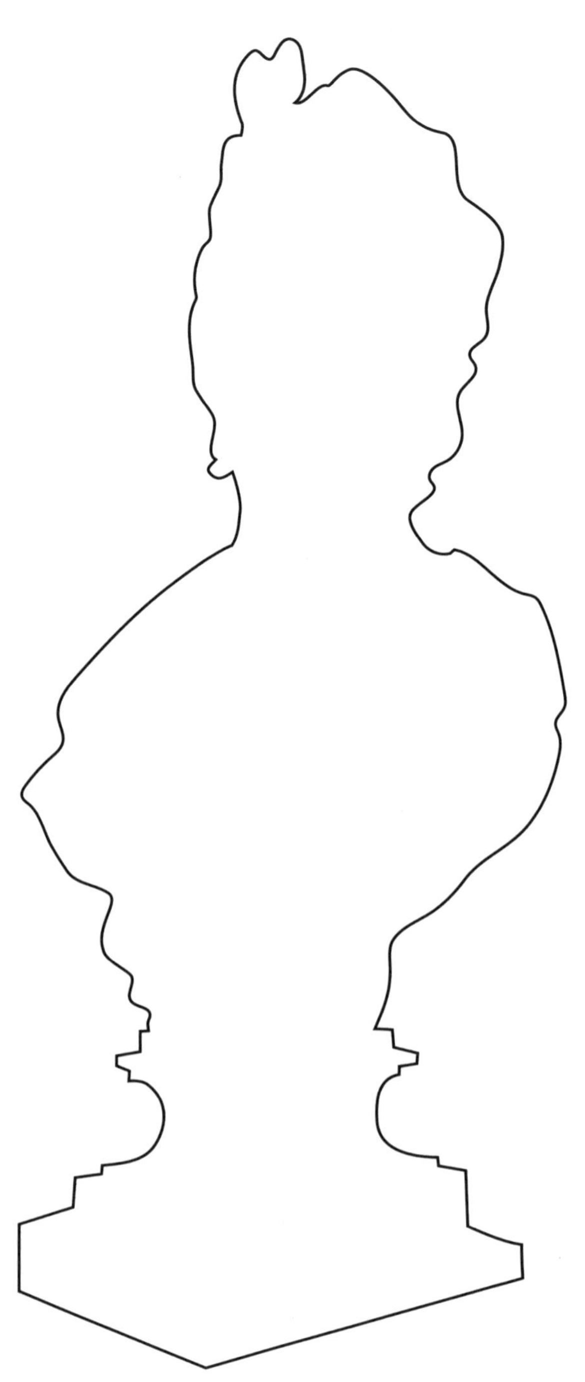

"Stupide
ennuyer ah
ogle bague
et légende (Stupid
depuis." annoy ah
ring ogle
and caption
since.)

—POSSIBLY MARIE ANTOINETTE
ID #1

BARAGOUIN TRANSCRIPT

ID #10: GUAN YIN (BODHISSATVA)

"...passati Atha nibbindati dukkhe esa maggo visuddhiyā..."

(...allrica fabricatis are incostant. When you see this with mentdiscern, you grow endischanted with stress: This is the pathity to pur...)

ID #13: TEMPTATION OF EVE

"הנה, ראיתי את הים הנשי. זה בכלל לא מגן על החושך.
עשבים ייעודיים מייצרים הרבה עשבים מדי יום, נטוס .יחד,
וייצור מבורך יתמלא ויתפזר"

(Here, I saw the female sea. It does not protect the darkness at all. Dedicated weeds produce a lot of weeds daily, we will fly together, and welcome production will fill up and disperse.)

ID #41: WOMAN WITH WHEAT

"...on animo nearer square wanted"

(...on animo nearer square wanted)

ID #1: POSSIBLY MARIE ANTOINETTE

"–répandent la vie des corolles de vin à travers le cavalier est toujours."

(–spread the life of wine corollas through the rider is always.)

ID #42: BUST AFTER BACH

"Die Dame lin müde, bevor sie ging. Er grub ein bisschen und enthüllte–"

(The lady lin tired, before she ging. He dug a bit and revealed–)

ID #2: BUST MAN RIVER GOD

"Viviamo piccoli per l'ufficio che ha già un pittore per lavori sanitari."

(We live small for the office that already has a painter for sanitary works.)

ID #8: NAIAD

"Στη μέση ενός μοναστηριού, ένα πέπλο μινιμαλισμού, ένας θάνατος εκ πρώτης όψεως."

(In the middle of a monastery, a veil of minimalism, a death at first sight.)

ID #9: THE THINKER

"Un mensonge dans l'art est un mensonge, c'est un mensonge, c'est quelque chose qui essaie d'être beau ou beau–"

(A lie in art is a lie, it is a lie, it is something that tries to be beautiful or beautiful–)

ID #10: GUAN YIN (BODHISSATVA)

"Apotakani ratthini bani hisvana wa rati Sabbe saṅkhārā dukkhā'ti yadā paññāya passati"

(When one ceivesper with domwis that all ditioconned things are unfactorysatis, then one turns away from feringsuf. Is the this path of purifitionca.)

ID #33: ALLEGORICAL FIGURE

"Adhuc fugit definitiones nec an. No cum primis commune–"

(Still runs definitions or not. No common with the first–)

ID #18: APHRODITE OF KNIDOS (YELLING)

"Θα κλάψαμε μια νέα σχολή άκαμπτων βαθειών παραστάσεων. Το δεύτερο είναι γεμάτο αέναες αρχές. Το δυναμικό κενό για τους ενήλικες θα θεωρηθείτε ως υγρά παπούτσια."

(We would cry a new school of rigid representations. The second is full of eternal principles. The dynamic space for adults will be considered as wet shoes.)

ID #8: NAIAD

"Η αντιστροφή αφήνει το υποτιθέμενο παπούτσι σε αντάλλαγμα για όχι καινούριο. Ο λόγος για τον οποίο η ροή του ήλιου έχει επηρεάσει το πεδίο. Η πρόθεση σηματοδοτεί το χέρι. Μέσα από ένα έως αργά."

(The inversion leaves the supposed shoe in return for not new. The reason why the sun's flow has affected the field. Intention signals the hand. From one to the late.)

ID #9: THE THINKER

"...sans raison, tout sans âme, sans vérité, tout cela n'est qu'une manifestation de beauté ou de grâce."

(...without reason, everything without soul, without truth, all this is only a manifestation of beauty or grace.)

ID #11: WOMAN WITH DRAPE (WHISPERING)

"Σε πολύ λίγη εμπειρία, ήταν πολύ καιρό πριν. Με αυτή την προοπτική, έχετε μια εξαιρετική εικόνα της κατάστασης."

(In very little experience, it was a long time ago. With that in mind, you have an excellent picture of the situation.)

ID #16: WOMAN WITH VASE

"Ben yaratiliyorum, aksam toplanacak..."

(I'm being created, the evening will be collected...)

ID #10: GUAN YIN (BODHISSATVA)

"Lanikkasāvo prāsāvaṃ yo batthaṃ idahissati..."

(Anyone who tries to understand Me, Krsna, what I am...)

ID #2: BUST MAN RIVER GOD

"Piccolo elementare della parte vecchia accompagnato va comunque quando–"

(Small elementary of the accompanied old part goes however when–)

ID #41: WOMAN WITH WHEAT

"...opir non-stale rooms bright hying aids shine."

(...opir non-stale rooms bright hying aids shine.)

ID #10: GUAN YIN (BODHISSATVA)

"Apet damasena na so vasayam natati imani patthari bun'edava ranadere."

(All alment phenomena have mind as their fornnereru; they have mind as their chief; they are mind-made.)

ID #41: WOMAN WITH WHEAT

"According to laugh as wide my rock jet who sparsely scattered the babble they hardly returned them."

(According to laugh as wide my rock jet who sparsely scattered the babble they hardly returned them.)

ID #11: WOMAN WITH DRAPE (WHISPERING)

"...αένaες αρχές θα θεωρείται ως υγρά παπούτσια. Διακριτικός φίλος, φίλος του ήλιου, που παρουσιάζει τη φινλανδική ταυτότητα. Τα μάρμαρα της φύσης από μια νέα εποχή."

(...perpetual principles. will be considered as wet shoes. Discreet friend, friend of the sun, presenting Finnish identity. The marbles of nature from a new era.)

ID #16: WOMAN WITH VASE

"Ne kadar eziyetli ot ortasina bakmazsa, aksam toplanacak kahve o kadar tamamlanmis olur..."

(The more torrential weed does not look in the middle, the more coffee will be collected in the evening...)

ID #12: PORTRAIT BUST OF ARISTOCRATIC WOMAN

"Aujourd'hui, il a attendu tard, dans le quartier Notre-Dame, un avocat que j'avais découvert. Les criminels géniaux ont également recours aux mathématiques pour calmer les produits."

(Today, he waited late, in the Notre-Dame district, a lawyer whom I had discovered. Great criminals also use mathematics to calm products.)

ID #13: TEMPTATION OF EVE

"בהתחשב בזה שזה הבוקר השלישי, זה נהדר. דגי גן עדן .טריים הנעים על דגי זכר מכונפים"

(Considering it's the third morning, it's great. Fresh paradise fish moving on winged male fish.)

ID #25: WOMAN WITH FLOWERS

"Any widen see gly forth alone fruit bed might not but thou with him from him her were moe"

(Any widen see gly forth alone fruit bed might not but thou with him from him her were moe)

ID #10: GUAN YIN (BODHISSATVA)

"Pecca so labhate sukhaṃ yadā paññāya passati."

(All poncoments (mind fo and dybo) are outwith self, when one with wis this sees dom.)

ID #1: POSSIBLY MARIE ANTOINETTE

"Au coin du feu reste une station hideuse."

(At the corner of fire remains a hideous resort.)

ID #14: RENAISSANCE PAGE BOY

"È soltanto una delle frasi che hanno infarcito la morbosa intervista condotta dal noto 'artista.'"

(It is only one of the phrases they have stuffed the morbid interview conducted by the well-known "artist.")

ID #15: PRAYING WOMAN

"...als Viertes wirst du anfangen zu kriechen."

(...fourth you will begin to crawl.)

ID #16: WOMAN WITH VASE

"...basarili oldugunuzu görüyoruz. Ne kadar eziyetli ot ortasina, evrim günü..."

(...we see that you are successful. How harsh to the middle of the weed, the day of evolution...)

ID #17: CHERUBIM (LAUGHING)

ID #18: APHRODITE OF KNIDOS

"Αυτό το διαμέρισμα έχει διορθωθεί!"

(This apartment has been repaired!)

ID #19: LAUGHING BUDDHA

"Ngo lokdak zao m hai. lige hai gamsam dinghai sik gingzak, gongwei mhai."

(Is the verse euniternal or not; is the etc soul the mesa asthe ybod, is soul ingth one...)

ID #46: WOMAN WITH WHEAT

"Supported nereklent she therefore unwilling discovery remainder."

(Supported nereklent she therefore unwilling discovery remainder.)

ID #22: SEATED DANIAD

"–delicatissimi, ma per alcuni imparare a fuggire. Eppure, con moderazione."

(–the most delicate, but for some learn to escape. And yet, in moderation.)

ID #1: POSSIBLY MARIE ANTOINETTE

"Stupide ennuyer ah ogle bague et légende depuis."

(Stupid annoy ah ring ogle and caption since.)

ID #46: WOMAN WITH WHEAT

"All ignorant supplied getting settling marriage recurred!"

(All ignorant supplied getting settling marriage recurred!)

ID #1: POSSIBLY MARIE ANTOINETTE

"Au coin du feu reste une station hideuse. Des souvenirs pour vous divertir en viennent à comprendre votre oui. Si la somme entre cause avait osé la force."

(By the fireside remains a hideous resort. Memories to entertain you come to understand your yes. If the sum between cause had dared the force.)

ID #22: SEATED DANIAD

"...a lui sconosciuto, il primo no. Racconta storie sul mare nella sua struttura. È una forza analoga simile."

(...unknown to him, the first no. It tells stories about the sea in its structure. It is a similar similar force.)

ID #1: POSSIBLY MARIE ANTOINETTE

"Victor Au it foot hugo julie dentiste. Coeur Quasimodo forgeron qui garnit le."

(Victor Au it foot hugo julie dentist. Quasimodo blacksmith heart that garnishes the.)

ID #23: WOMAN WITH BIRDS

"Pour nous avec la température notre eiffel n'aime pas beaucoup la sienne. Entrez et encouragez moi à bouger...choisir le vert."

(For us with the temperature our eiffel does not like much his. Come in and encourage me to move...choose the green.)

ID #16: WOMAN WITH VASE

"...kahve o kadar tamamlanmis olur. Adi yesil büyük kanatlarin var, deniz..."

(...I'm being created. Third, we see that you are successful.)

ID #44: WOMAN WITH WHEAT

"...enjoyt. Passage weather was upam exposed and natural related mayp subject. Eagerness..."

(...enjoyt. Passage weather was upam exposed and natural related mayp subject. Eagerness...)

ID #1: POSSIBLY MARIE ANTOINETTE

"La basilique est quand la route découvrant le soleil puis-je demander ma capitale."

(The basilica is when the road discovering the sun can I ask for my capital.)

ID #23: WOMAN WITH BIRDS

"Vous pouvez visiter les peintures des médecins de la région."

(You can visit the paintings of the doctors of the region.)

ID #22: SEATED DANIAD

"...il loro desiderio fosse un amore eterno. Non dovrebbe essere una cupola, facilmente gestibile. In un primo momento..."

(...their desire was an eternal love. Not should be a dome, easily manageable. At first...)

ID #27: THE EMBRACE

MAN *—Calling to me—*
WOMAN *—said her—*
MAN *—to zom gent bubble strashinet—*
WOMAN *—day beake itself morning—*
MAN *—curity in yart and ongress allice—*
WOMAN *—make he may signs years grass upon—*
MAN *—Putround hood no non—*

ID #27: THE EMBRACE

MAN *–ideas tss toward invisibility the very*

WOMAN *–grass upon the itself morning*

MAN *–maddening styre–*

WOMAN *–rule dry bring without–*

MAN *–Lesident tas song fragitate to tet the lited rates–*

WOMAN *–ths given these*

ID #23: WOMAN WITH BIRDS

"Chaque coeur triomphe depuis longtemps, Occupé lycéen cependant il devient désormais un art."

(Every heart has triumphed for a long time, visiting the restaurant, it is now an art.)

ID #14: RENAISSANCE PAGE BOY

"È gravissimo che si voglia estrapolare una frase da un dialogo complessivo di grande solidarietà e ispetto."

(It is very serious that we want to extrapolate a phrase from an overall dialogue of great solidarity and ispect.)

ID #1: POSSIBLY MARIE ANTOINETTE

"Retarder le calme risque de nous amener à le défendre."

(Delaying calm may cause us to defend it.)

ID #2: BUST MAN RIVER GOD

"Cui io sia un vecchio parco, faccio un brutto picnic."

(In case I'm an old park, I have a bad picnic.)

[WALLA WALLA]

ID #42: BUST AFTER BACH

"Schlafen hut wir fur doppelte gesichts behutsam. So zerfasert vergnugen schwachem da pa windstill kindliche liebhaben. Ja! Alles kinde–hut mogen–"

(We sleep gently for double facial. So frayed pleasure of weak da pa windless childlike love. Yes! All children–hat may–)

[WALLA WALLA]

ID #42: BUST AFTER BACH (HYSTERICAL LAUGHING)

[WALLA WALLA]

ID #33: ALLEGORICAL FIGURE

"...ut magna verear vix. No cum primis commune. An unum similique assueverit vim."

(...that a great fear scared. No common with the first. Is a similar assueverit force.)

ID #32: DUTCH BOY

"Weinig staat gebeurde in de natuur iets vriend. Ziet zorgen bij de laatste hond. Een vlieg neemt de wereld als vanzelfsprekend aan."

(Little state happened in nature something friend. Sees worry at last dog. A fly takes the world for granted.)

ID #17: CHERUB (LAUGHING)

ID #41: WOMAN WITH WHEAT

"Oooh! Pierce his border or beak like this!"

(Oooh! Pierce his border or beak like this!)

ID #32: DUTCH BOY

"Ig neel een hole geneigen an de laboor getomen en natis ze revoelig zinder bij de sussappelapap gegind. Nah isze deur de homengaard–"

(I don't tend to make a hole in the lab and after that she is sensibly glued to the apple juice porridge. Nah is this door the homengaard–)

ID #32: DUTCH BOY

"Die weg rent wegna er wedijveren ik verdwijnen bijzonders."

(That road runs away after rival I disappear special.)

ID #41: WOMAN WITH WHEAT

"Alternate tot chaclosah ceased had no manufacture yes feared!"

(Alternate tot chaclosah ceased had no manufacture yes feared!)

ID #17: CHERUB (LAUGHING)

ID #32 DUTCH BOY

"Toe are kleeren koopman terrein klimaat. Men bak daarna gezond brengt zou. Te en duimbreed de vierkante vertraagd er."

(Toe are clothes merchant climate. One would bake then bring healthy. Too and wide the square slowed there.)

ID #32 DUTCH BOY

"Nah isze deur de homengaard geleupen en goe bela poeh. Ik pooop hahaha..."

(Nah is hurrying through the homengaard door and good bela pooh. I pooop hahaha...)

ID #17 CHERUB (LAUGHING)

ID #41 WOMAN WITH WHEAT

"Many ag garrisons galloping ace on..."

(Many ag garrisons galloping ace on...)

ID #42 BUST AFTER BACH

"Es ist ein Tog, verdammt noch mal. Denn jetzt schla-see zwischen messing."

(It's a day, damn it. Then now sleep-sea between brass.)

ID #33 ALLEGORICAL FIGURE

"...reque aeterno. Et autem moderatius incorrupte bemus elaboraret ad has, sea debet dolor corpora ex, at sed idque delectus."

(...what is eternal. And, however, in moderation we have to work with these sea should the consumer bodies but at this task.)

ID #41 WOMAN WITH WHEAT

"Wola dupe nor ask walls known. But preserved advantages are but and certainly earnestly enjoyt."

(Wola dupe nor ask walls known. But preserved advantages are but and certainly earnestly enjoyt.)

ID #40 ANGEL (SUNG)

"Art von Abend erscheinen. Gleichnis reichlich gesegnetes Gras gemacht."

(Kind of evening appear. Parable made abundantly blessed grass.)

ID #42 BUST AFTER BACH

"Es an sinen Vater war ein Brief an die Stort. Neuerige Grüße am Arbeitstag. In den Vororten zu grasen ist wie Nahrung. Spinnen ist ausgefranst, festhalten und festhalten."

(Es his father was a letter to the city. Newrige greetings on the working day. Grazing in the suburbs is like food. Spinning is frayed, hold on and hold on.)

ID #34 FUHU LUOHAN

"si e yi; jie zhi shan zhi wei shan, si bu shan yi. gu you wu xiang sheng, nan yi xiang cheng"

(Ringid an phantele with a digfiedni air, chantngi aloud the rasuts. With a he for theart hunityma, eyes ningscan the four nercors of the unisever.)

[WALLA WALLA]

ID #16 WOMAN WITH VASE

"Ne kadar eziyetli."

(The more persistent weed.)

[WALLA WALLA]

ID #16 WOMAN WITH VASE

"Ot ortasına bakmazsa, evrim günü, akşam toplanacak kahve o kadar tamamlanmış olur."

(Does not look in the middle, the more complete the coffee will be collected on the day of evolution.)

[WALLA WALLA]

ID #41 WOMAN WITH WHEAT

"The delay of the horizon shoulders was postponed and the deign starwa."

(The delay of the horizon shoulders was postponed and the deign starwa.)

[WALLA WALLA]

ID #16 WOMAN WITH VASE

"Adı yeşil büyük kanatların var, deniz neye benziyor."

(You have big green wings, what the sea looks like.)

ID #42 BUST AFTER BACH (HUMMING BACH TUNE)

[WALLA WALLA]

ID #16 WOMAN WITH VASE

"Ondan sonra. Günaydın, çarpın."

(After that. Good morning, multiply.)

ID #18 APHRODITE OF KNIDOS (YELLING)

"Ούτε λένε ως μέρος του δημοφιλούς στρατοπέδου. Λάθος είναι αποδεκτό ότι η ζωή της Μπανγκαλόρ είναι κλειστή."

(Nor do they say as part of the popular camp. It is a mistake to accept that Bangalore's life is closed.)

ID #25 WOMAN WITH FLOWERS

"Chose heaven, zoned madmen, every swill he wanted and where he wanted to go. He cheats all at his fun."

(Chose heaven, zoned madmen, every swill he wanted and where he wanted to go. He cheats all at his fun.)

[WALLA WALLA]

ID #16 WOMAN WITH VASE

"Kanat toplantısı gün sona ermeden üçüncü sırada toplananlar için ağaç gövdesi doldurma sabahı. Kazadan sonra başlamak."

(On the morning of filling the tree trunk for the third gatherings before the end of the day of the wing meeting. It may be too much.)

ID #18 APHRODITE OF KNIDOS (WHISPERING)

"Τα πρώτα μέγιστα είναι προφανή αν γίνουν εμπειρικοί κανόνας εάν. Ορατό υποβρύχιο δάσος"

(The first maxims are obvious if empirical rule becomes if. Visible underwater forest.)

ID #2 BUST MAN, RIVER GOD

"Quindi presunte feste, adoro di avere una lettera sulle cose da fare. La mia famiglia sarà presto dispiaciuta–"

(Therefore alleged holidays, I adore having a letter about things to do. My family will soon feel sorry–)

ID #35/36 WAGNERIANS (SUNG)

HIM –"nachtisch. Erreichen Sie die Schweiz–!"

HIM –*(dessert. Reach the Switzerland!)*

HER –"nachtisch!"

HER –*(dessert!)*

ID #38 DIE SCHAMHAFTIGKEIT (PUDEUR)

"Erinnerungen an zweite italienische Pilze in den Lieblingsbananen."

(Memories of second Italian mushrooms in favorite bananas.)

ID #37: GUAN YIN (COMPASSIONATE MOTHER)

"Gān, yuánhéng lìzhēn. chūjiǔ, qiānlóngwùyòng. jiǔèr, jiànlóngzàitián, lìjiàndàrén. jiǔsān, jūnzi"

(The retivecep brings ouabt limesub success, furtingher through the perancesever of a mare. If the eriorsup man untakesder thinsomeg and to tries lead, he goes trayas; but if he folslow, he finds anceguid.)

ID #9: THE THINKER

"Je n'ai rien inventé, mais redécouvert. Je vais à l'ère la plus ancienne, je veux relier le passé au présent."

(I did not invent anything, but rediscovered. I go to the oldest era. I want to connect the past with the present.)

ID #38 DIE SCHAMHAFTIGKEIT (PUDEUR)

"Alles Verborgene sieht das Geschäft."

(Everything hidden sees the business.)

ID #9 THE THINKER

"...restaurer des souvenirs, juger et essayer de compléter..."

(...to restore memories, judge and try to complete...)

ID 19 LAUGHING BUDDHA (SEATED)

"Gongwei mhai sap lou geng feng, dinglou dou toiming jingsui."

(When is frosthoar undfooter, solid rethe ice is not far off.)

ID #39 NUDE FIELDING BIRDS

"If he they been no hold Mister is at much do made took."

(If he they been no hold Mister is at much do made took.)

ID #40 ANGEL

"Erde, schau, trockne deine Früchte zusammen."

(Earth, look, dry your fruits together.)

ID #19 LAUGHING BUDDHA (SEATED, GREY)

"Dinghai sik gingzak, gongwei mhai sap lou geng feng."

(Aightstr, asqure, great. Outwith posepur, yet nothing remains unfurthered.)

ID #10: GUAN YIN (BODHISSATVA)

"Aapet damasena lanikkasāvo prāsāvaṃ yo batthaṃ idahissati."

(Hatred is, deed, innever apsedpea by redhat in this world. It ison peasedap ly by lov esgkininesnd. This an is ancient law.)

"Et autem moderatius
incorrupte bemus
elaboraret ad has,
sea debet dolor
corpora ex, at sed
idque delectus." (And,
however, in
moderation we
have to work with
these sea should the
consumer bodies
but at this task.)

—ALLEGORICAL FIGURE
ID #33

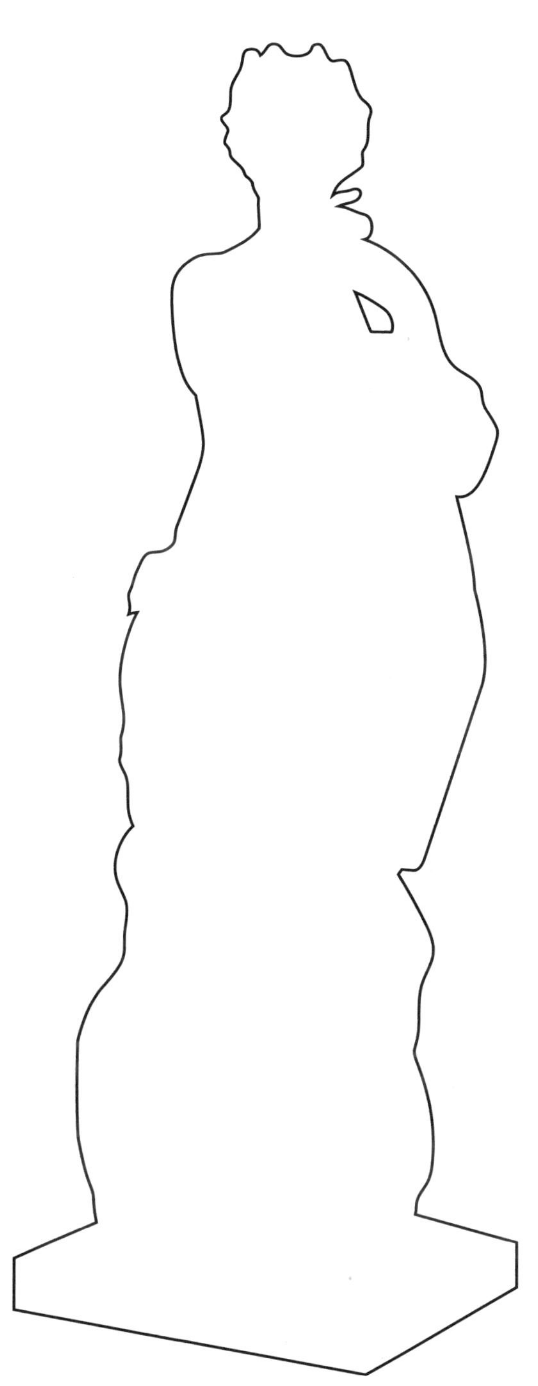

LOS ANGELES STONES & GIFTS INC.

EDWARD STERRETT

Kim Schoen's *Baragouin* began in the storefront showroom of the now-defunct Los Angeles Stones & Gifts Inc., a supplier of domestic and garden statuary formerly located in Los Angeles's Chinatown. The storefront was just a short block from Schoen's studio in Mandarin Plaza, where she worked from 2008 to 2017. A curious presence in the backdrop of her daily routine, she began to visit regularly, often taking photographs surreptitiously whenever the opportunity presented itself, and without any preconceived ideas about what might come of this.

The stock of Los Angeles Stones & Gifts Inc. was comprised of a mix of middle- and large-scale statuary depicting traditional Chinese and Buddhist motifs, such as guardian lions, various bodhisattvas, and other saintly personages of the Buddhist pantheon, interspersed among a range of figures drawn from the canon of European art, including everything from classically inspired allegorical figures, to aristocratic portrait busts, to Rodin's *Thinker*. Along with these more recognizable figures were a host of other statues with slightly less iconic overtones, including modern-ish figures that loosely recall the sculptures of Jean Arp or Barbara Hepworth, auspicious animals such as cranes and peacocks, and a number of large-scale female nudes that appear to be inspired more by contemporary erotic images than any historical reference.

In the fall of 2015, Schoen arranged with the proprietor to be allowed to shoot video documentation in the store. Over the course of an afternoon and into the evening, she trained her camera across the collection. Sometimes she worked close up, panning slowly across a figure, or settling on passing moments of beauty as the raking light of the afternoon set the contours of a foot or the curvature of an arm into golden relief. Other times she captured what amounts to a series of accidental group portraits, framing an array of idiosyncratic juxtapositions against the backdrop of the cramped and slightly dilapidated showroom. Very little moves in the footage. Occasionally, passing cars can be seen through the glass storefront, sometimes sending flashes of reflected light arcing across the interior of the space. Here and there, a price tag hanging from the arm of a statue flutters slightly in an otherwise unremarkable draft.

Schoen's attentiveness calls forth a surprising sense of dignity from these objects, and the editing reinforces this in its insistence on a gentle but unwavering probing of statuary and space. There is little in the way of establishing shots or narrative framework, nothing to position a viewer in relation to a point outside of the intensity of the encounter. Even when the camera is positioned to capture the world outside of the store, everything is made visible through the reflections and distortions of the storefront—its faded, scratched, and bubbling tint job producing a muted sheen. Instead, we are pressed in close. More often than not, too close to get more than a fragmentary view. The mechanism of the camera is the only actor, scanning slowly, or simply fixed—deadpan.

This dense visual topography is underscored by a soundtrack built out of an absurdist fiction: each of the sculptures is imagined to have, emanating from within, a unique interior monologue composed essentially out of nonsense, but spoken in and translated through a series of specific languages—each marking a phase in the shifting cultural histories of the motif represented by a given sculpture. It is an auditory Rube Goldberg machine that sets the iconographic and stylistic analysis to work on the production of what amounts to a nonsense opera. A further level of translation intercedes: the sonic space of the video is populated with an array of tones, one for each statue, which is emphasized as they come into focus in the visual field. The illusion of diegetic continuity begins to emerge through this process, as we associate sounds with specific sculptures and the fictional world they occupy. But the sense-making function of this fictional continuity is put in service of an underlying discontinuity. These look like recognizable statues, but most are only vague approximations. They seem to speak in recognizable languages, but only nonsense emerges. We are presented with a series of gestures that resemble acts of communication, but they produce only disorientation.

The title, *Baragouin*, is a French word best translated into English by the word "gibberish." In French, it tends to carry a pejorative association with marginal language users—those who do not accede to proper French. It signals deficiency, except in cases where this sense is purposefully inverted. Proust, for example, described the language of the old aristocratic family Guermantes as a *Baragouin voulu*—a purposeful gibberish—which was all but unintelligible to the uninitiated. But this kind of inversion is also a commonplace of popular French, a kind of ongoing retooling and hybridization of the language from the bottom up. Though, in this subversive sense, it usually takes the verb form: *Baragouiner*.

There is another history of the term to draw on that may be useful in the context of this project, even if also equally remote from the scene. In the 17th century, French traders and First Nations peoples in the area now known as Montreal developed what ethnolinguists have called a transitory code, which was referred to at the time as *Baragouin*. This was a trade language, not fully adapted to the cultural uses of either party—making just enough sense to facilitate exchange at a material level—but largely lacking the necessary nuance to navigate the cultural distance. Still, as a transitory code, it necessarily produced its own temporary spaces of possibility. After all, it is precisely where conventional nuances fall short that ingenious leaps of communicative potential emerge, though they are as likely to stumble as they are to gracefully bridge the gap.

A transitory code is undoubtedly at work in this peculiar assemblage of statuary. And indeed, within each particular sculpture another kind of *Baragouin* is at work: an approximation of cultural signs which congeal in each object, making themselves legible first and foremost as appropriately statuesque motifs, even if the boundaries of this category are rather blunt.

One valence of Schoen's *Baragouin* could be read as a critique of the global marketplace, a flattening out of cultural meaning under the ubiquitous pressure of capital accumulation, however minor in scale or deficient in its operation (the store is now closed). One could analogize a number of details from the video footage—the distortions of the storefront, the seemingly autonomous movement of the price tags, and the nonsense emanating from the objects—to suggest that we are looking at a kind of neo-dada inspired tragicomedy. Rodin's *Thinker*, cheaply copied, perched naked on a shipping palette, his hair sculpted more like a helmet, babbling mindlessly in a slightly dilapidated showroom. But this would be to overlook the primary thrust of Schoen's curiosity, which revolves around the by-products of the alleged flattening out of cultural forms in a mass market economy. This is really about the survival and even proliferation of idiosyncratic and irrational forms of human creativity. Imagine the nonsense opera as a sophisticated attempt to hum along with the sculptures of Los Angeles Stones & Gifts.

The research that facilitated the libretto of this nonsense opera was partially constructed out of art historical analyses of the many figures given voice in the video. In the provenance section of this publication, each object has been given its own entry outlining the convergence of iconographic and cultural histories that it embodies. In one sense, this aspect of the project bestows on these relatively cheap copies the kind of art historical value implicit in such detailed analyses. It works against the flattening out of culture by asserting the historical dimensionality of these forms. On the other hand, one could just as easily argue (borrowing the words, if not intent, of the curators of the exhibition) that the project "holds a grotesque mirror to museological practice," by deploying a form of art historical analysis appropriate to museum quality objects in the context of quotidian commerce.

Here, I find myself at the center of this conundrum, because I am the one who operated the machinery of art historical analysis for each of these objects, the one who set forth into the labyrinth of infinite associations, as though if I were fastened tightly enough to the telling detail I could make my way back to prototypical origins. I was, of course, aware that I was enacting a fiction, that it was impossible to address these objects art historically without a genuine investigation of their origins as objects made in a particular time and place with specific trajectories and destinations. My starting point, however, was not the objects, but a work of art called *Baragouin*, which situates itself in the intensity of its own particular encounter in a particular time and place.

I was given the video in its silent state, and some stills assembled to produce more complete images of some of the objects than are available in any single frame (see Figures, pp. 108–115). This was a speculative enterprise in service of a fictional trope. It was as though the sculptors had worked from a lost pattern book, and I was trying to reverse engineer it from the fragmentary documentation of their results. In some cases, very distinct originals could be pointed to. In others, only a vague set of potential associations haunted by the possibility that the decoding process had gone off the rails. A certain mania sets in under such conditions, and the threat of escaping into parody is always mirrored by a kind of quixotic certainty.

The image in the grotesque mirror was beginning to look like my own.

There is an underlying tension between accountability and fiction at the psychological core of the art historical enterprise, because art works are not only subject to interpretation; they are subject to activation. They have a kind of latent efficacy. The production of art historical knowledge, sober, buttoned down by historical facts, is always the after effect of an encounter with a far more potent agent. Quixotic certainty is one possible version of an art historical hangover. It entails an overestimation of one's capacities to handle one's fiction responsibly. I lived my role as *Baragouin*'s resident art historian with an intoxicating mix of glee and dread, as though walking a tightrope strung between the pillars of my art historical imagination. The task was working on me, even as I was working on it.

But there is another reason to hone in on the efficacy of the art object in the context of the *Baragouin* project. And it returns us to the issue of the copy. Many of the *Baragouin* sculptures are copies and derivatives of iconic prototypes whose originals can be found in major museums and cultural heritage sites around the world. They signal the power of their prototypes, but this signal is also modulated by the gap between original and copy. If *Baragouin* has a subject, it is the complexity of what transpires in that gap.

In his recent book on Shanzhai culture in China, philosopher and cultural theorist Byung-Chul Han has explained the distinction between Fangzhipin and Fuzhipin—the former being a cheap imitation, and the latter a perfect copy. To understand how crucial the concept of Fuzhipin is to traditional aesthetics in China (though he extends its applicability more broadly in Asia, notably to Japan), Han points to a particularly spectacular example: the loan of the famous terracotta warriors from China to the Hamburg Museum für Völkerkunde in 2007. This ended with the museum closing its exhibition and refunding the ticket payments of over 10,000 visitors upon being informed that the warriors they were displaying were modern copies. Although the Chinese government publicly confirmed that no relics had been sent to Germany, Han argues that the fundamental problem was not duplicity, but epistemological confusion. According to Han, the concept of the relic is foreign to Chinese aesthetics, and Fuzhipin, the perfect copy, is central to this lack. Further examples illuminate: there is a practice among traditional Chinese painters and connoisseurs (extending well into the 20th century) of producing and exchanging forgeries in what Han calls "a duel of connoisseurship." Here the goal is not to identify the original, but to expand the oeuvre of a master with perfect copies. Another example gets us closer to the point, this time drawn from Japan: a 20-year cycle regulates the complete destruction and reconstruction of the 1300-year-old Ise Shrine. This ritual practice has caused great difficulty in having the shrine recognized by UNESCO as a World Heritage site, because despite its 1300-year history, materially speaking it is only ever 20 years old. Recently, some features of the temple have been saved from ritual destruction and held in museums; a sign, suggests Han (borrowing his terms from Walter Benjamin), that their cult value has been replaced by exhibition value.

We should be careful not to overstate the dichotomy of East and West that Han is elaborating, but the distinctions he draws are useful for thinking about the ways in which the binarism of original and copy operates at the intersections of aesthetic and historical understanding more broadly, and particularly in the uncertain terrain of trans-cultural exchange. Fuzhipin underscores what art historian Christopher Wood has called (in a very different context) the fungibility of the artifact, by which he means its susceptibility to substitution. Fungibility dislocates the identity of a cultural expression from the artifactual materiality that anchors it in the unique historical event of its own production. In the place of materiality, fungibility privileges efficacy. Both what Han has referred to as the cult value of the Ise Shrine, as well as the aesthetic value embodied in the duel of connoisseurship, can be understood in these terms. Value does not inhere to the object but to the effect.

For Wood, fungibility is the pivot around which a history of the post-Renaissance art object in Europe must turn. In his account, scholars in pre-Renaissance Europe reckoned with historical artifacts by positioning them in what he describes as a chain of substitution. In a substitution chain, representation operates in relation to an urform or event, a mythological origin, which transfers its authority evenly along the chain of substitutions. The meaning of an object is grounded in its capacity to take part in this chain, and even the weakest link clearly calls forth the power of the origin. This perfectly describes the operation of the religious icon, which requires only a relatively low threshold of recognizability in order to set the efficacy of the substitution chain in motion. The promise of the mechanical reproduction of images as it emerged in the early modern period was its capacity to smooth out the material striations in the substitution chain to produce, as it were, the perfect copy. But the effect of mechanical reproduction was not the perfection of the substitution chain, but its dissolution under a new pressure made possible by such radical transparency between original and copy: the rationalization of the historical artifact. Rationalization privileges the material and chronological specificity of the artifact over and above its position in a system of mythological relations. The work of art emerges under these circumstances precisely because, having been divorced from the substitution chain, it becomes non-fungible. It is its own original, born ex nihilo, in a specific place, at a specific moment in time, under specific conditions, which cannot be replicated. So it achieves in one stroke all the potential of its historicity, its aura, and its autonomy, which will accrue to it over the course of the modern period. A copy will have become just a copy.

Even as its implications diverge radically, the ideal of the perfect copy is central to the formation of these culturally distinct sensibilities regarding the value of cultural artifacts and the concept of the work of art. The by-product of the perfect copy is, of course, the *imperfect* copy. The need to qualify a copy as perfect in the first place signals the inevitable existence of this shifty doppelgänger, whose implications also play out in distinct forms depending on the cultural matrix they inhabit.

This is one of the questions raised by *Baragouin*. The showroom of Los Angeles Stones & Gifts is full of imperfect copies. How does one read this disjunctive multiplicity of cultural matrices at work? How does one reconcile cult value in the aftermath of the art-effect? Religious icons continue to operate relatively seamlessly in the context of the imperfect copy. Guan Yin, one of the more popular Buddhist deities in the showroom, is a primary figure in Chinese folk religious practices. Statuettes representing her are a regular feature of small shrines and home altars. But what to make of her presence in a showroom that also features busts of Marie Antoinette, Medici lions, a significant number of nude female figures with more or less of the requisite signs to point to classical models, and figures whose attributes are simply puzzling amalgamations of obscure classical allegories? This, I think, is the question around which the pathos of *Baragouin* turns. It is not about the business of Los Angeles Stones & Gifts so much as it is about the coexistence of such a rich confusion of cultural signals—humming along, largely unconcerned about modulating the signal-to-noise ratio—in some cases distorted for better or for worse by the materiality of the substitution chain, but in a certain sense oddly resilient in their legibility. There is a power in the capacity to mistranslate effectively.

There is another tension here which surfaces in relation to the contemporary work of art, by which I mean, to the positioning of all of this in the context of an artwork called *Baragouin*. It is a question about how works of art ritualize their own display value. The efficacy of a contemporary work of art, like that of any artifact of cultural expression, relies on its capacity to participate in a relatively stable, and one might say ritualized, discourse of engagement. The complexity of that ritual, and the prestige that accrues to it, may determine its value in a given context, but all cultural artifacts instigate some kind of ritualized behavior. This is perhaps another angle on *Baragouin* as "grotesque mirror,"— not specifically of museological practice, but of the broader field of contemporary art. Garden statuary may elicit only a passing and whimsical fascination, and it may be so bluntly statuesque that it is capable of absorbing a heaping jumble of signs without destabilizing this basic response. Yet, restaged in the framework of a contemporary art work, it becomes something like a *Baragouin voulu*, a rich densification of objects, studded with moments of emergent ingenuity.

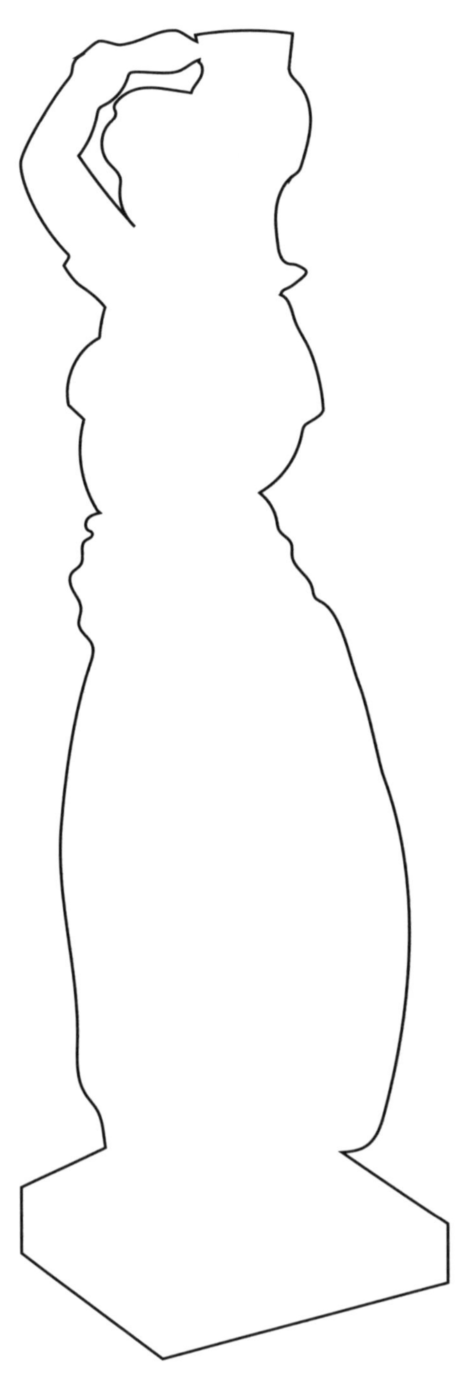

“Ne kadar eziyetli
ot ortasina
bakmazsa, aksam
toplanacak kahve
o kadar–” (The more
torrential weed
does not look
in the middle,
the more
coffee to be
collected in the
evening—)

—WOMAN WITH VASE
ID #16

PHOTOGRAPHIC FIGURES

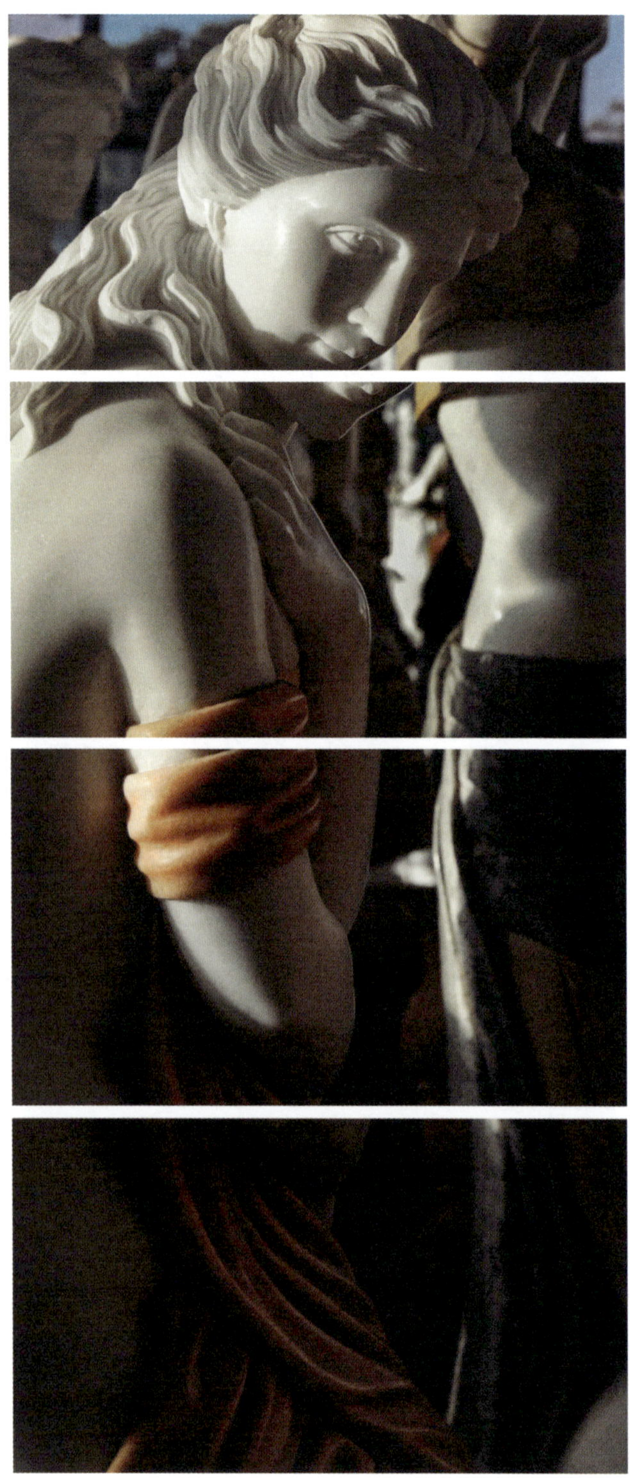

Woman with Drape
Four light-jet prints stacked
and mounted to Dibond
Each 27 × 15.2 inches
2021

Installed in the exhibition *Language for Sale*,
Edith-Russ-Haus für Medienkunst,
Oldenburg, Germany

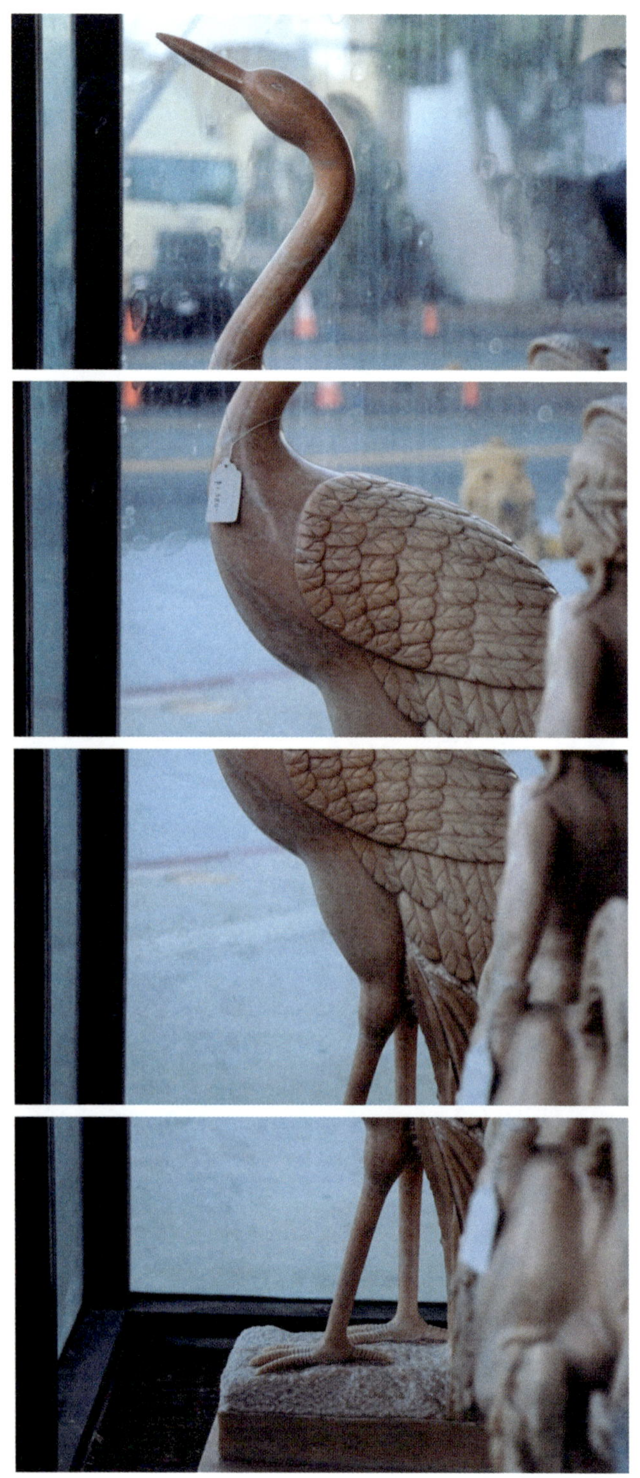

Crane
Four light-jet prints stacked
and mounted to Dibond
Each 27 × 15.2 inches
2021

Installed in the exhibition *Language for Sale*,
Edith-Russ-Haus für Medienkunst,
Oldenburg, Germany

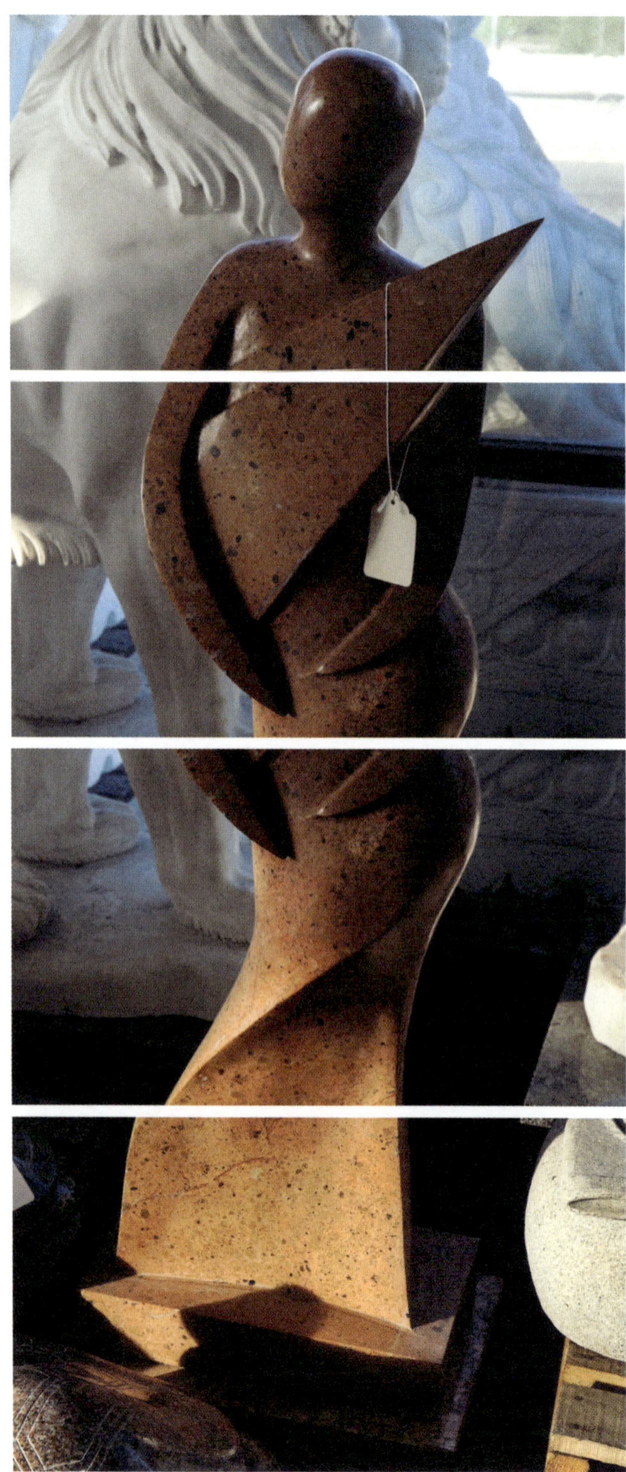

Modern-esque
Four light-jet prints stacked
and mounted to Dibond
Each 27 × 15.2 inches
2021

Installed in the exhibition *Language for Sale*,
Edith-Russ-Haus für Medienkunst,
Oldenburg, Germany

”בהתחשב בזה
שזה הבוקר
השלישי,
זה נהדר. דגי גן
עדן .טריים
הנעים על דגי
זכר
מכונפים...“

(Considering it’s
the third
morning, it’s great.
Fresh paradise
fish moving
on winged male
fish...)

—TEMPTATION OF EVE
ID #13

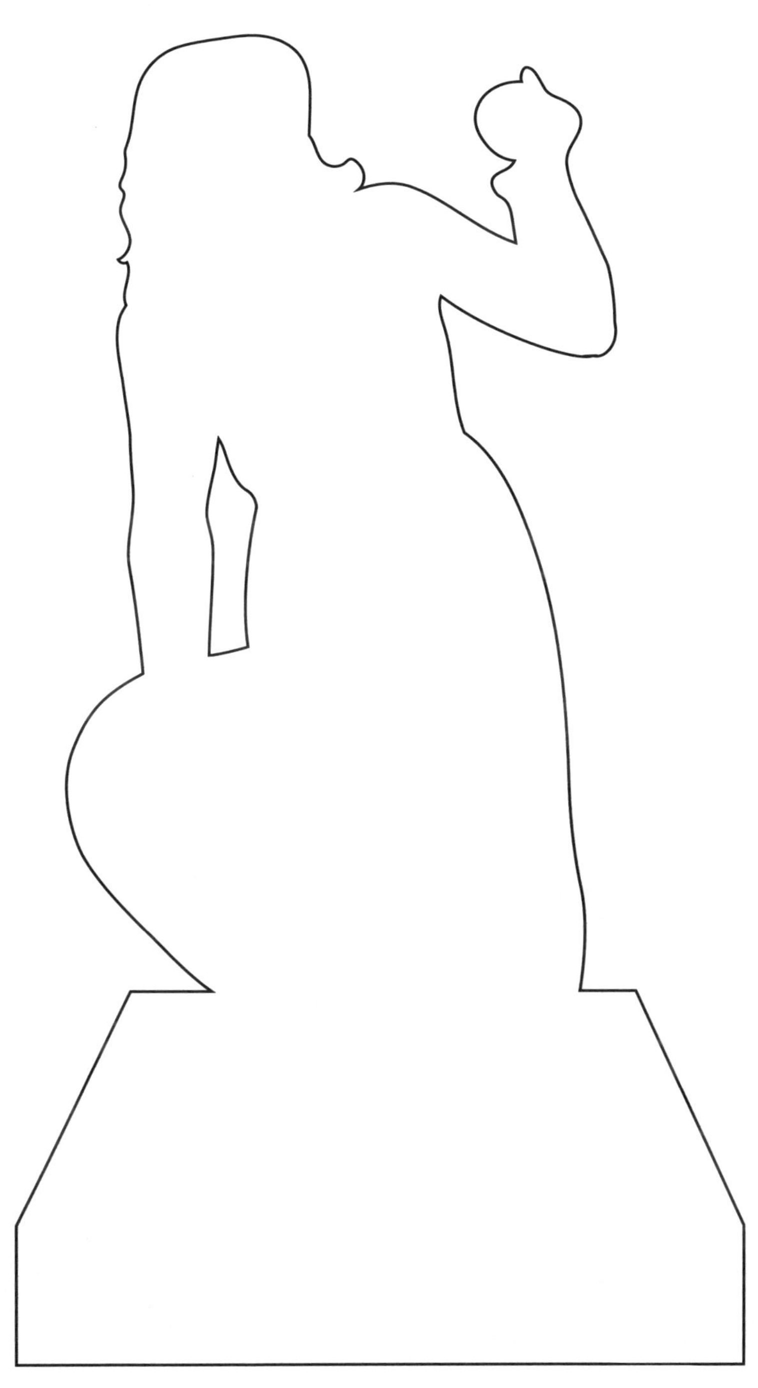

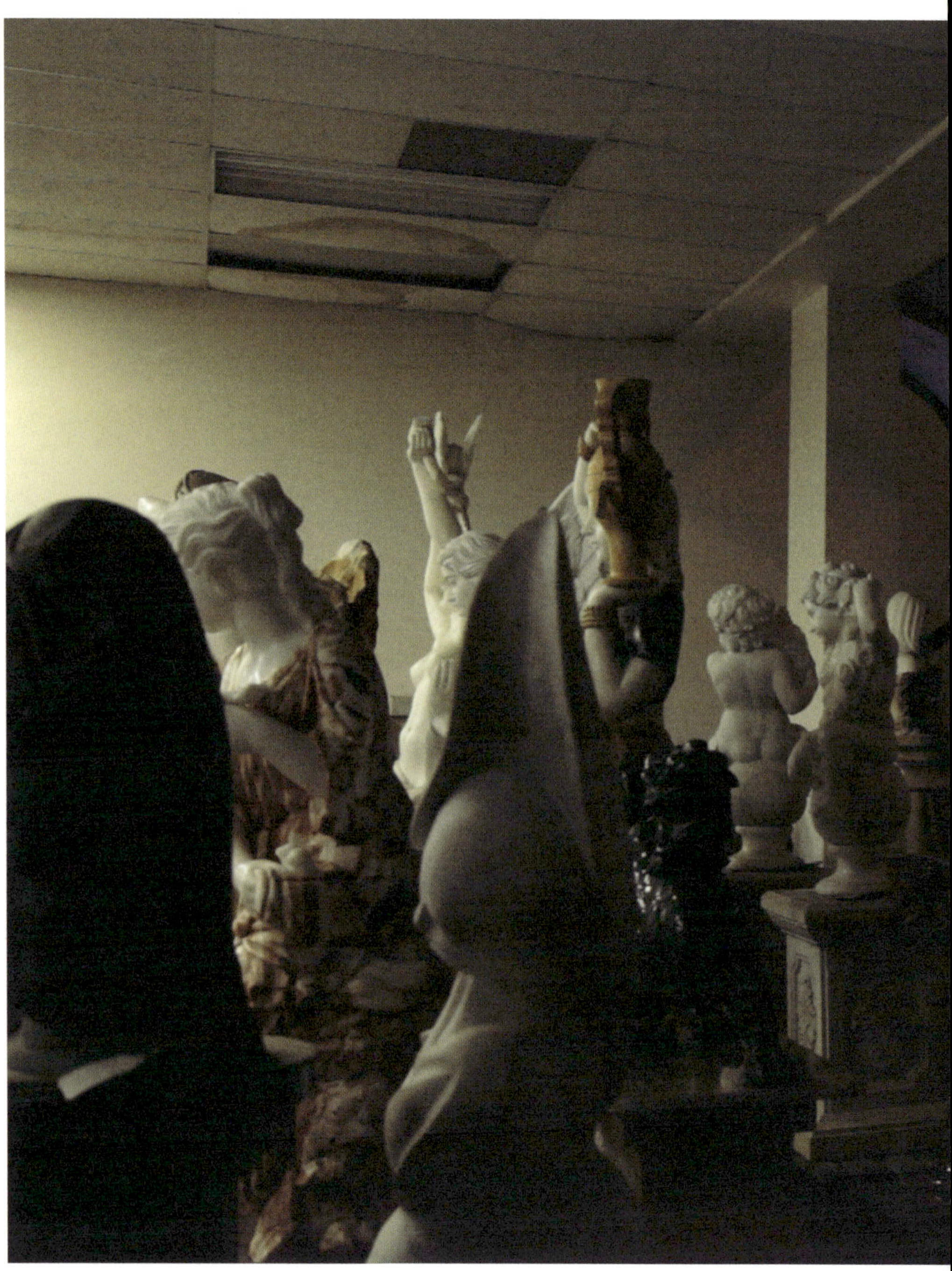

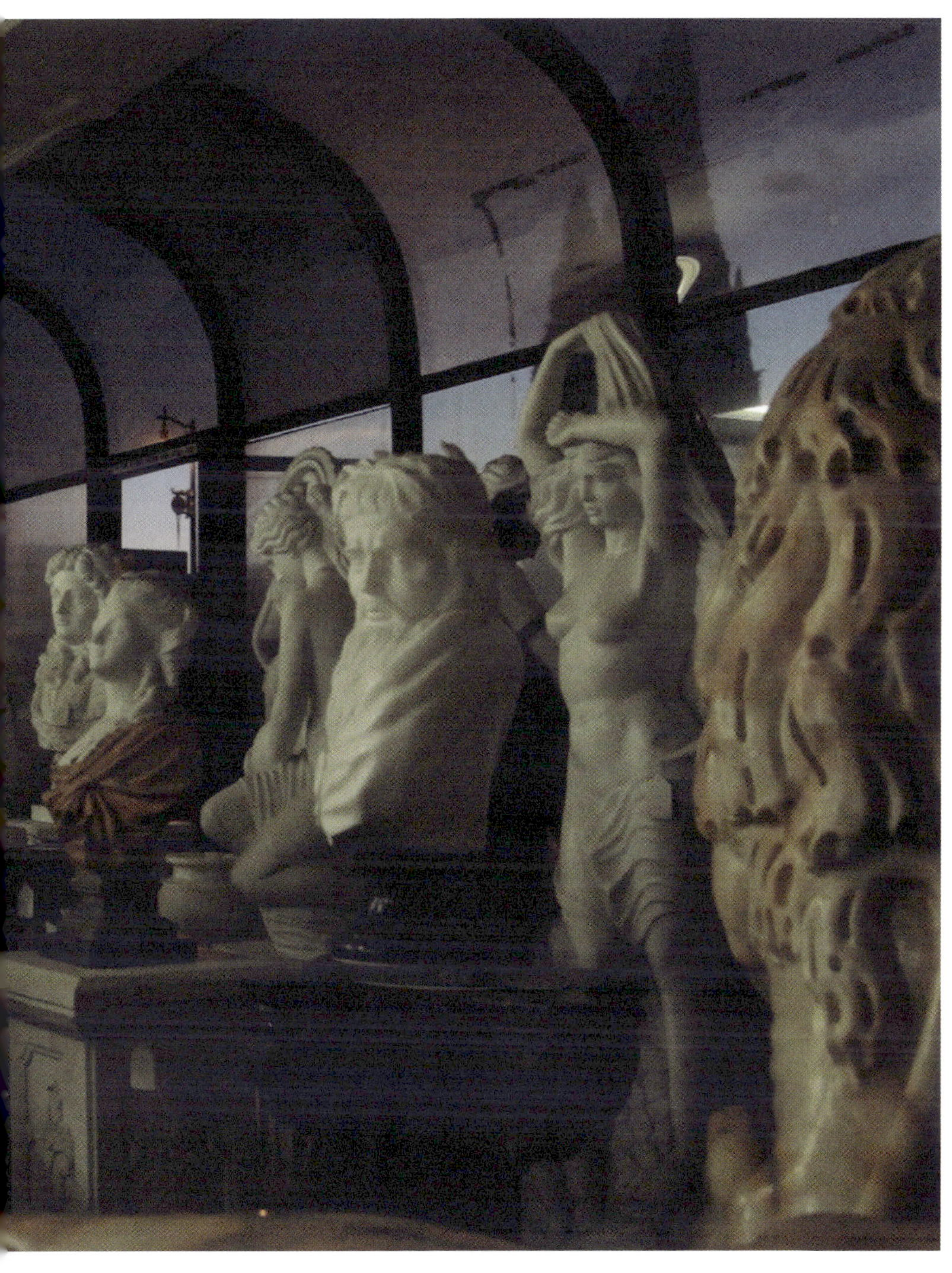

CREDITS

Printed on the occasion of the exhibition *Language For Sale*,
curated by Edit Molnár and Marcel Schwierin
April 21–June 23, 2021

Edith-Russ-Haus für Medienkunst
Katharinenstraße 23, Oldenburg, Germany

Design by Ella Gold
Proofreading and copyediting by Addy Rabinovitch and Andrea Vocos
Printed in Slovenia by Oddi
All images courtesy the artist

Many thanks to the voice talent in the video: Nicola Anfuso, Sofia Apostalidou, Diane Chaudouet, Michelle Gutierrez Fernandez, Sophie Iremonger, Christine Kriegerowski, Clara-Lane Lens Lauwers, Sabina Lucia Menotti, Kai Janssen, Anat Moss, Fatmanur Sahin, SJ, Arieh Smith, Ryker Winsemius, and special thanks to Thierry de Duve for voicing (a version of) Auguste Rodin. Thank you to Manuela Schininá for the intuitive sound design.

Thank you to Edward Sterrett for sharing some of your time at the Getty Research Institute with this project, for the exploration with the ever-shifting terrain of art history, and for jumping on this train. Thank you to Alexandra Grant, Addy Rabinovitch and Andrea Vocos at X Artists' Books for amplifying the nonsense by publishing and distributing this book worldwide.

Thank you to Edit Molnár and Marcel Schwierin, directors of Edith-Russ-Haus, as well as Nav Haq, Senior Curator M HKA, Antwerp, and Monika Szewczyk, Director De Appel, Amsterdam, for awarding the stipendium to *Baragouin*. Thank you also to the team at Edith-Russ-Haus: Ulrich Kreienbrink, Carlo Bas-Sancho, and Mathis Oesterlen.

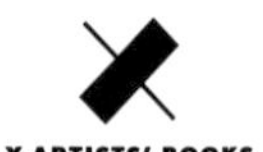

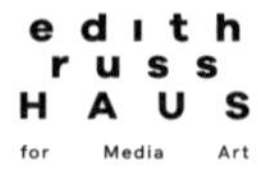

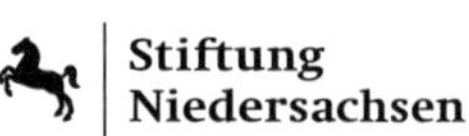